LIFE IS MORE
THAN 9 INNINGS

LIFE IS MORE THAN 9 INNINGS

BY FRANK SULLIVAN

Memories of a Boston Red Sox Pitcher

Published by Editions Limited
PO Box 10150
Honolulu, Hawai'i 96816
www.hawaiipublisher.com

Library of Congress Cataloging-in-Publication Data
Sullivan, Frank
Life is More Than 9 Innings – Memories of a Boston Red Sox Pitcher
1st Ed.
I

ISBN 978-0-915013-54-8
Softcover, First Edition 2008
Printed in China

Cover illustration: "The Rookie" by Norman Rockwell was on the cover of the Saturday Evening post dated March 2, 1957. I have my arm on Jackie Jensen's shoulder as he ties his shoe. Ted Williams is standing behind Jackie. Far right is Billy Goodman and sitting left foreground is Sam White. The "rookie" is Sherman Safford who at the time was a fine local high school player. John J. Anonymous stands on the left. Read more about it on page 74.

Dedication

This book is dedicated to the greatest gentleman I have ever known.
He was my biggest fan and my best pal and the reason this all got down on paper.
This book is dedicated to Leal Sullivan, my dad.

LIFE IS MORE THAN 9 INNINGS

Forewords

I first met Frank Sullivan at an NFL Alumni golf tournament in Kona, Hawaii, in 1978. We were trying to play a game we both loved, golf. For 18 holes I listened to story after story, from a man that I watched play when I was a young man; it was while he was with the Boston Red Sox. I knew that day that Frank should tell his story.

What you're getting ready to read is history. Not only some great baseball stories but the lessons of life through a life that was lived the way it was supposed to be lived. Frank Sullivan is one of the most intriguing people I have ever met. I have been honored to call him a friend.

> — June Jones
> Head Football Coach, University of Hawaii 1999-2007

Friendship may have as many definitions as there are people. For most of us, we have far more acquaintences than friends. Frank is one of the very few who seems to have tipped the scale in the opposite direction. While the book is clearly an often amusing, sometimes poignant, journey through his life, the underlying opportunity is that each of us may learn how to follow Frank's lead.

> — Tom Shapland
> Chicago, Illinois

His writing is fresh and appealing because it is honest. It brings back memories, that is for sure, but it also transcends time because his words tell us about people, how they feel and react, and that really doesn't change.

> — Joseph Kennedy
> Pupukea, Hawaii

On the back of his 1950s-era baseball card, the one that came with bubble gum and was endlessly "flipped" on playgrounds across America in that decade, it states "Frank writes short stories as a hobby." Well these are the shortest stories of all American authors, fiction or otherwise. According to Frank, they were written for the "horizontal" reader, implying that they are of such a length as to allow one to read a single page and fall asleep in bed. This is the perceived perfect length for the modern-day reader of such tales. These poignant, yet infinitely entertaining, chronicles will take you on trips through locker rooms and sand traps, inter-coastal waterways and Hawaiian harbors. They will delight and astound you.

> — R.W. Duggan III
> Wimberley, Texas

LIFE IS MORE THAN 9 INNINGS

Preface

I started writing all of these one-page stories you are about to read because of a moment in time when my father was staying with us. Just my wife and I were having dinner with him. He was 86 years old at the time and the everyday conversation had waned. For some unknown reason, as I finished my last bite of food, the thought occurred to me I really didn't know a damn thing about my father other than the years I had growing up under his wonderful touch. So I simply asked him the simple question I should have asked years before. "Dad, what was your life like before you met Mom?"

It was if I had torn the top off a new box of goodies. It was like opening a rare bottle of wine. It was what I should have asked when I was old enough to talk.

Leal Earl Sullivan was, as I knew him up 'til then, a quiet, proud, hard working man of great resolve. If every child had a father like him there would be no wars. But being asked the question, he shocked me with his response. He lit up like a bonfire and started a three-hour life tour that had Marilyn and me laughing and crying and spellbound. For me there has never been a better night and, as I lay in bed with his young life still ringing in my ears, it dawned on me that I, too, had led a special life and someday my kids and grandchildren might want to know.

So I started to write a few things I remembered and the more I wrote the more I remembered. Soon I realized I really wasn't writing all this for them as much as I was writing it for my own pleasure. I decided on a one-page format so I wouldn't be guilty of rambling on and also because that's about all I can read in bed before a book hits me in the face anyway. I remembered an autobiography by Jack London that preached if you were going to write then you better write every day and throw away most of what you write.

You are now stuck with what I didn't throw away.

> — Frank Sullivan
> Lihue, Kauai
> May, 2008

Opposite: Just as they snapped this picture of me and Ted Williams, he was asking me why I had a bat in my hand. He really knew how to hurt a guy. Maybe it was my lifetime batting average of .144!

LIFE IS MORE THAN 9 INNINGS

Introduction

As I look back on the many satisfying things I have done on this wonderful trip through life, I can't deny that a ten-year Major League Baseball career is one of them.

The Combat Infantry Badge, framed on my wall above this spot where I write, is dear to my heart because it is a symbol of my not being labeled a coward.

High school seems so far back, but I was the Student Body President of Burbank High (enrollment 2,000 plus) for a year.

I retired my parents and got my father out of the cannery where he worked so hard as an independent contractor responsible for all the stacking, labeling and the making of boxes and took them east to let them see me pitch for the Red Sox.

Then there was the late night at the Colonial Country Club in Lynnfield, Massachusetts. I borrowed Jimmy Baltas' brand new Cadillac on a freezing night to get back to the Kenmore Hotel in Boston. Suddenly, I skidded off onto the median strip when the pavement went to ice, hurting the front alignment of the car. I'm still proud of the fact that I bought Jimmy a brand new exact copy the next day and had to borrow the money to do it. (The repaired one went to my dad.)

Very little surpasses the satisfaction of building a boat; the waking in the night to assume the working out in the mind of how to cut the angles of a design that has no square corners, the excitement of each solution, the fitting of the joints to assure they are strong and sound and when the craft is launched, it performs the required tasks. I couldn't live without a boat in my yard and when boredom rears its ugly head, and I believe boredom can kill, there is always something I can do to my boat. Hell, just dragging it around to a new spot in my yard makes me feel good all over.

People might say I have been lucky because I was able to sustain a life here in paradise but, in my own defense, I was always up for the task. I willingly gave my best effort to whomever would hire me and never with a dollar in mind. I have always felt that money is a product of success and not a requirement for it.

And, yes, I am vain, although most of it went away in 1964 here on Kauai when Sam White and I put on a baseball clinic in the town of Hanapepe. I was on the mound at their municipal park and Sam was catching and a young boy (about 8 years old) standing next to me while I was showing them how to come, set and hold a man on first base asked me, "Mr. Sullivan, who did you play for?" "The Red Sox," I answered. He looked down at the ground and said, "Yeah, me too." Out of the mouths of babes, eh?

I bet he feels better, like I do, because our team won the World Series in 2004.

Opposite: I don't know who the kid was or how he got on the field but at the time it was just two ballplayers talking about the game.

Simply put, I've had a hell of a good life. I've seen Niagara Falls bathed in flood-lights and been to the Rock Islands of Palau. Watched the sunset in the lee of Niihau and been to the Military Tattoo at Edinburgh Castle. Sailed to Matthew Town, Great Inagua, and pitched in a Major League All-Star game. Surfed the bowl at Hanalei when it was overhead and was a friend of Henry Hinckley.

I've been in every major city in our country and seen the ice bergs breaking away from Greenland. Spent a year in Japan and a week in Alaska. I've played the Old Course at St. Andrews and heard the noises in the Everglades at midnight. Been in Madrid at siesta and watched a Spitfire take off from the grass runway at Dux-ford. Sailed the East Coast from Halifax to Key West and been to Yap.

I've lunched with Arnold Palmer and been on the cover of the Saturday Evening Post. Skied at eleven thousand feet and been across Lake Mead in a very small boat. Was skin diving when you had to cut your mask to fit and drove a car across our nation in three and a half days, alone. Les Brown's "Band of Renown" played at our high school prom and I was on a boat when we caught 96 tuna in one day.

I sat in the company of Joe DiMaggio to hear Sinatra sing with the Tommy Dorsey Band at the Palladium and drank with Ralph Evinrude on his yacht. Been to the rain gauge at the wettest spot on earth and watched Ted Williams hit his last home run in his last at bat in Fenway Park.

I've seen Loch Ness and have been to Ponape. I practiced all winter with the Boston Celtics the year Bill Russell came to the team. I remember Southern California when there wasn't any smog and knew Jim Murray as a friend. I've sailed under the Golden Gate Bridge and past the Statue of Liberty. Been upside down in an open cockpit and traveled to Truk. Was a guest at the Culloden House in the Highlands and stood atop the Empire State Building.

I've been to Hatchet Bay, Eleuthera, and taken the tube in London. Attended the Masters Golf Tournament in Augusta and flown to Kwajalein. Seen the Rock of Gibraltar and had my picture taken with Ed Sullivan. My home town honored me with a parade and I got paid to play ball in Mexico.

I spent five days at a Trappist Monastery in Hokkaido and played golf on the Algarve coast. Drank many nights with Henry Tai Hook at Black Pot and walked the Boardwalk in Atlantic City. Talked to Bob Hope in the Red Sox dugout and watched Kilauea erupt at midnight.

With all that said, the best thing I ever did was marry the girl with whom I live on this beautiful island of Kauai.

The Painted Baseballs

The painted baseballs that are used at the beginning of each chapter are the work of Del Wilber.

Del was a back up catcher when I joined the Red Sox in 1953. I had no idea that he had a hobby of painting a ball depicting each game won by a pitcher on the team and presenting the ball to the pitcher a few days later. As one can imagine it was a wonderful surprise and the term, "I missed out on a Wilber ball" was used to admit a loss by all of us pitchers.

Each ball was numbered to match the number of wins it represented for the hurler. Then there was also the box score displayed and highlights of the game where there was room on the ball. Naturally, the 8th win got you an 8 ball painted all black just like on a pool table.

Unfortunately, Del was at the end of his career and was gone in the middle of 1955 I think. When he left, other players tried to match his idea but all failed in regard to content and color.

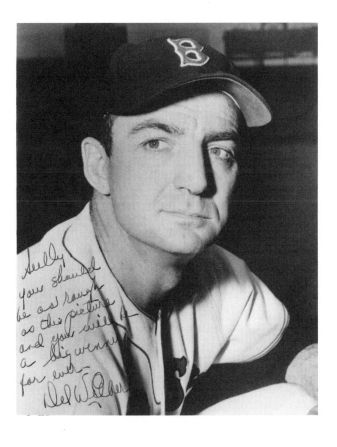

Table of Contents

Growing Up

In the Army

Early Years in Baseball

In the Big Leagues

Reflections on the Game

After Baseball

A Moment in Time

Sullivan by the Numbers

GROWING UP

Let me introduce you to my sister Carol. We are still as close as this picture portrays.

Calling Me Home

From the first time my sister Carol was instructed by my father to "call the boy home," she called me "boy."

At first, I had no idea what the "BOY!!! COME HOME BOY!!!" yelling was all about. I was up the back alley with my buddies throwing rocks at something and wondering who was calling and who they wanted to come home. A few calls later I heard my dad roar, "HEY BOY, YOU BETTER GET HOME RIGHT NOW!"... OK! OK! Now I knew! And so it started, in 1935, that my calling home was done by my sister and from that moment forward, she called me "boy" no matter if it was in private.

My buddies were quick to point out that it seemed to be my sister's wish that I get home. I wondered why she was the one who had to call? Why didn't I get a call from a higher authority over the years than by my two-year-younger sister? Jesus, it was embarrassing to be playing on the street in a heavy game of kick-the-can and have a tiny but very loud assertive voice start her cadence call. "Boy! Boy! You better get home now!"

Hey! In those days it was hard enough to resist authority because of the inevitable discipline that resulted. Then again, if you were having a great time (winning at anything) you had to assess the chance that it might not be a bad spanking if your father had a good day at work, but to have your baby sister calling you home without mentioning your real name was humiliating. Pretty soon the guys would start chiming in, "Hey you. What's your name? Oh yeah, 'boy,' you better go home boy because your little baby sister says so!"

My parents took us to the World's Fair in San Francisco in 1939 and crowds of people were dumbfounded with that same call. Parents were looking around like maybe all the boys should assemble or something. I was peddling a swan boat on a lake built on Treasure Island when the call "Boy! Boy! Come in Boy" came resounding across the water. Everyone on that lake heard it and the whole scene came to a grinding halt waiting for someone to confess the call was for them. It was hard to pretend I didn't know who the call was for and, with my dad standing next to her on the shore, I was toast.

I love my sister (always have) and I don't remember when my name stopped being "boy" or why, but I am more than glad she isn't calling now. She would probably be calling "Old man! Old man! You better get home now!"

If it was the same wonderful house we lived in then, I might go.

My Love of an Unpaid Job

In the news of late (May 2007) are wild fires surrounding Griffith Park and I'm sure that those fires have been a terror to the people living around that long time recreational area bordering the mostly dry Los Angeles river bed turned into a concrete wash and the mountains that separate the valley area of Glendale and Burbank from the Pacific Ocean plain. If you walk over those low mountains you are in Hollywood.

Years ago I found a job in that public park that thrilled me. It was at the big merry-go-round. I was the kid that refilled the brass ring dispenser. During the ride, I would swing out the dispenser close enough for a rider in the outside lane of the beautifully painted horses rising and falling to lean out and grab a ring.

Once they got a ring, they looked to see if it was the brass one with the free ride. If it wasn't they threw it back into a cage-like structure that would collect the steel rings into a small pocket and that's where I would collect them, fill the dispenser and be ready for the next ride. I mean was that an important job or not? Add the fact that if the rides were full, I might put two brass rings in the mix without a word of reprimand.

I would get home at night totally spent and satisfied and couldn't wait to do it again. I remember how important I felt and how I couldn't imagine anyone else doing it with the same dedication and expertise.

My memory says I got the job while my family had a party there and I was kind of bored and walked around the backside of the huge structure to find a kid doing a sloppy job with the ring thing. I pitched in and as soon as he felt my enthusiasm he left me alone and the burden felt good. No one saw or deemed the position change but it was mine as I saw it. I think I was maybe 7 or 8 years old.

It ended after a few days when my mother said she wasn't about to take me all the way to Griffith Park again. I was crushed. I explained to her how important the job was and that I felt committed to see it through. I talked of how easy it was for me to get it done right. I also admitted that my being able to hop on and off the big rig as it went around without having a ticket made me feel important. I bared my soul!

Well, it was to no avail. My mother sat me down and explained the ugly facts. First off was the fact that I had never been hired. Secondly, the family could not afford to take me to the park every day of that summer and finally, I needed to understand that any kid could do a job that doesn't pay anything. I cried myself to sleep.

Too bad there isn't a big merry-go-round in a nice park here so I could finish the job that was made for me.

Parking Lot Job

Billy Thompson's family owned the Thompson Dairy in Burbank, California just across the railroad tracks from the Lockheed aircraft manufacturing plant where all the P-38 fighter planes were built, along with the Lockheed Lodestar bombers in WWII. In fact, they took a lot of pasture land and made a giant parking lot to accommodate the cars of some of the thousands who worked there. The plant was going full blast 24 hours a day with 30,000 people each 8 hour shift. Their huge dirt parking area filled up three times every 24 hours and at ten cents a car, the parking lot did somewhat better than the cows that would have been there.

It was 1942 and the entire plant and runway were completely covered with a camouflage netting and from above it looked like a golf course. I always thought it must look quite odd to a spy plane to see all the cars in the parking lots that were constantly filled right by the golf course. Maybe a 24 hour tournament?

One summer I worked there collecting parking fees on the first morning shift. Now pay attention and you'll have a new profession to fall back on. You wear a coin changer with a pocket apron. In your left hand between the thumb and fore finger you put a dime and a nickel. Under the middle finger, a quarter. Under the last two fingers is a half. OK? The cars will rarely stop unless they need change for a $5 or $10 bill. Here is how it went. If the person had a quarter in his hand, you took it and put it in your apron pocket with the right hand and gave the thumb and fore finger (.15) in your left hand. If the person gives you .50, you gave them the thumb and fore-finger and the next finger (.40) and, finally, if they gave you a dollar you gave them the whole hand full of coins. Always going back to the changer to replace what you gave. Which is all great but has nothing to do with the story I intended to tell you.

Billy was given a horse for working at the parking lot. It was a very large (17 hands) white stallion which he named "King." Nothing to do every day after collecting dimes but go over to the corral and try to break (tame?) the huge creature. To this day I still believe that 12-year-old people should not be allowed the pleasure of bringing to rein a beast of that size and temperament. It seemed to me that "King" was always pissed. To this day I question my own sanity and reasoning that allowed me to sit on top of the fence and willfully throw myself atop the animal as he ran by while Billy was staggering up out of the horse manure and dirt. My mother would question me when I got home each day. "If you're working at a parking lot, why do you come home smelling like something your father would like to put on the lawn?"

My Biggest Fan

I was 13 years old and in John Muir Junior High School in Burbank, California. I was your typical kid, full of hell and looking for more. Although I had stopped throwing rocks at other kids (tough repercussions), there was still an aggressor in me that longed for action. I found it on the playground and, like it or not, athletics was very satisfying to me. Yes, it took me a while to learn to lose. I learned crying solved nothing and if you are not willing to lose, you can't possibly win.

Looking around, I realized there was something some of the other guys had that I didn't. Money! These guys didn't play sports after school or rarely during it, but they had money and went to the picture shows and soda parlors whenever they felt like it and never lacked for girlfriends. The one thing all these guys had was a job.

So, I went looking for a job and skipped playing ball after school one day. I had heard a service station down by the railroad tracks was looking for an after-school worker to pump gas, check oil and tire pressure and clean windshields.

I had never asked for a job before. The first one I had, and the one that is still listed on back of my Social Security card, was as a delivery boy for the Burbank Advertiser and they had asked me. I liked the idea of throwing papers and wearing the newspaper canvas paper holder that was two pouches divided by a hole for the head. You were given some bundles of newspaper and then you had to fold them so they could be thrown a good distance and this meant a tight fold was best. When you got through throwing the papers in the front pouch, you simply pulled the back pouch to the front and went about your business throwing, while riding your bicycle up and down the hills of Burbank. Throwing while going downhill was the most difficult because of the speed of the bike and one mistake with too much effort throwing and you were coleslaw! The porches were the targets.

At any rate, to my surprise, I was hired by the gas station owner and he said for me to start right then. Well, I wasn't prepared for that, but I did take the job and was next to useless. Hell, I didn't know you had to turn the air pump on, nor did I have a clue where the oil dip stick was on each different car. I was embarrassed when the owners of the cars had to get out of their vehicles and show me.

I wasn't on the job an hour when my dad drove up in our 1936 Oldsmobile. He motioned for me to come and get in the car and off we went toward home. Without looking at me, and with measured words, he said slowly that if I wanted to work it would be for him, but he preferred I didn't. He said he wanted me to continue playing sports and he would work harder to make sure I had a buck in my pocket. It was easy for me to succeed in sports; my dad was my biggest fan.

Jim Stroud and I, wearing our Burbank High letterman sweaters, enjoy a laugh with Bunky Alpin.

A Snake on the Porch

Johnny Kirkpatrick, Cliff Smith, Buddy Day and yours truly were intent on ridding the foothills of mountain lions. We were 15 years old. I had never seen one, but given that Buddy lived in the very den of those hated creatures, La Tuna Canyon, north of Burbank, we couldn't wait to hunt down the beasts and put them to their rightful end. I was lent a 22 rifle 4-10 shotgun over-under and, to this day, search for a gun like that beauty.

The night before was spent "camping" in Buddy's yard. We had made a hunting blind and spent some intense hours just after dark sitting waiting for one that had been harassing their chickens, but the need for sleep overcame that notion. About 1:00 a.m. the dogs started barking and there was a commotion around the chicken coops. I forget where I hid.

We marched off in the morning tracking the beast of last night by following the droppings up the ridge directly behind the house. We then lost the trail some mile or more still going up the foothills of that area. We hiked and hiked to the limit of our egos and finally decided to go the hell home. I don't remember who, but one of us said, "well, down is the quickest." It was also the dumbest, as we paid the price of traveling down a steep dry stream bed ravine that was strewn with loose boulders and took twice the time it would have if we had followed our path back.

As the sun faded from the foothills, we wearily marched back toward the homestead in fading light on a two-tire rutted dirt road. It was dotted with cow pies (that's cowboy talk for "doodoo") and one of the pies hissed and rattled at us. Johnny, being the closest, jumped back and we all let go with our weapons and blew that poor sucker to eternity. The rattlesnake was about four and a half feet long and was still in one piece. It was then that Buddy decided to take it home and try to scare his dad.

When we got to the house, Buddy coiled the rattler on the top step of the stairs of the front door. Buddy's mom made us a big dinner and we could hardly get it down waiting for his father to arrive. We sat on the edge of our seats when we heard his car come into the yard. Even Mrs. Day was amused.

All of us watched the door knob being turned and couldn't believe it when Mr. Day walked into the dining room unaffected. He smiled and nodded to us and sat down at the table rubbing his hands together and said, "I sure am hungry." We sat stunned. Then Buddy, no longer able to stand it, started for the door to see what had happened to the snake and his dad said, nonchalantly. "If you're going out son, be sure not to step on the rattlesnake."

Diving Helmet Trial

Johnny Kirkpatrick thought he could make a diving helmet out of a ten gallon can. Anything mechanical was out of my league, but I trusted Johnny to create our next diving experience. Johnny produced the helmet and I was there in his garage (just the two of us) when he explained how it should work. The can was padded and rounded for the shoulders and had straps under the arms to keep it on. There was a rectangular piece cut out for the glass window with an innertube as a gasket. There was a fitting which he soldered above the glass window for a long hose attached to a bicycle pump. Seemed right to me and we took off for Laguna Beach. We were sixteen.

It was a dismal, grey day and no one was on the beach. Johnny put on the helmet which made him look like a bad movie. The first try we made was scrubbed because the helmet alone was not enough weight to keep him walking on the bottom. So, next try was with a large boulder that we dug out of the side of the highway where we parked the car. It had to weigh at least 60 or 70 lbs and did, in fact, keep him submerged as he strode out into the small surf carrying the damn thing. I stood at the water's edge pumping the bicycle pump to keep him supplied with air as the hose played out behind him.

All seemed to be going well until I realized I was running out of hose and he was still wandering out into yet deeper waters. I didn't want to yank on the hose because Johnny had said the fitting above his face that supplied air to the helmet was the weakest part of the whole scheme. Nothing to do but follow him out until I was holding the pump at chest level above the waist deep water and pumping was more difficult. Surely Johnny would realize there was only so much hose? Surely Johnny would understand that Franky could only pump the pump so many times before collapse? Surely Johnny would realize that by now I was holding the pump high in the air and trying to use muscles that were not up to the task. Surely HELL! My arms collapsed into the water and I closed my eyes knowing that my friend just drowned.

Not so. Being no dummy, Johnny let go of the boulder and up popped the helmet. He released the arm straps and freed himself from the contraption. His face was covered with black oil. He could not see and called for me to guide him as he struggled to swim my way. The oil we had lubricated the pump with had gone the whole distance to his helmet and came in right over his face and darkened his world. After he got his face cleaned up he said, "Let's go home and I'll modify this and next time it's my turn to pump." I didn't bother to reply.

Upper left is Cliff Smith. Johnny Kirkpatrick and Buddy Day are to the right and the revised diving helmet is put on display by Buddy.

New and Improved

To test the "new improved diving helmet," Johnny Kirkpatrick enlisted Buddy Day, Cliff Smith and yours truly. The four of us regularly went skin diving off the coast of Southern California in 1946. In those days you bought a face mask made out of hard black rubber about a quarter of an inch thick and literally cut the edges to fit your face. We took the new helmet, made from a water heater, to Hansen Dam located at the head of the San Fernando Valley. The first helmet, made from a ten gallon can, was scrubbed because the air intake was over the forehead of the diver and the bicycle pump we used deposited the lubricating oil into the eyes of the wearer. This time Johnny used a very light coat of Vaseline to grease the pump and relocated the air intake valve behind the head of the wearer.

To keep the diver down, Johnny had fashioned a belt with window sash weights. We took two inflatable life rafts so the pump could be handed back and forth from Johnny to Buddy and they could alternately pump and rest. Cliff was to be the diver. You knew it wasn't going to be me, right?

It was decided that we would launch the rafts first and then Cliff would walk into the lake. I had a mask and fins on and swam along to keep the rafts positioned over Cliff, who promptly disappeared below into the murky green water. As I watched from the surface with my mask, it seemed to me it was dropping off too fast and, in fact, I saw Cliff stumble a couple of times before he disappeared completely into very tall lake weeds. It wasn't long before I raised my head out of the water while holding onto one of the rafts and said, "Cliff just disappeared into some slimy green weeds that reach up over his helmet."

Johnny said, "We haven't got a whole lot of air hose left so go down and motion for him to turn around." I swam down following the air hose. The top of the helmet was barely visible, deep in the weeds at least fifteen feet under the surface. I could just imagine what was going through Cliff's mind as it must have been scary as hell with all that slimy stuff on him. If I didn't have fins on it would have been hard to get down that deep and as it was, I didn't have a lot of air left when I made the mistake of tapping on the top of the helmet.

Cliff, perhaps thinking he had been attacked by the lake monster, let out a loud yell which I couldn't help from laughing at and which blew all my air out. Somehow I got back to the surface without blacking out for lack of air and Cliff, who had enough for one day, dropped the weighted belt and let the air in the helmet take him to the surface.

When Cliff got out of the contraption he looked at Johnny and said, "I hope those weren't special sash weights." "Naw, Cliff," Johnny replied, "I don't need to open the windows in my room anymore."

Outside Loop Problems

I grabbed the hand-hold and stepped into the toe-hold allowing me to leg over into the back open cockpit of a Stearman bi-plane (two wings). For those of you who don't know, a cockpit has nothing to do with chickens, it is a hole in the top of the fuselage of a airplane that lets you sit on a very uncomfortable piece of metal and be able to look out forward through a windshield. There is no lid!

Only if you are very old will you remember a film named "Dawn Patrol." It portrayed WWI pilots living the good life and risking their lives to kill the HUN. I especially remember the landings of those planes that didn't have air brakes. They side-slipped to reduce speed just before touching down. Are any of you with me? Let's just say I had always wanted to fly in an open cockpit plane.

In 1948, Johnny Kirkpatrick and I drove north to Oxnard where he knew of a pilot who was trying to make a living ($8 per ride) scaring the hell out of people. Johnny went first and I watched in awe as the plane did everything all over the sky but fly straight. When it landed, Johnny climbed down from his flight with a look on his face that should have given me a clue, but youth must be served!

I settled into the hole in the fuselage and the pilot, standing on the lower wing, took one look at me sitting on the seat set at Johnny's level (we differ in height by about a foot) and said, "First, tighten your seat belt then pull the lever on the left side of the seat and adjust it to where you'd like it." I pulled up on the lever and the seat dropped all the way down to the bottom position which fit me just fine. Unfortunately, he did not ever say to me that there was another move to be made to lock it down. I'll bet you're with me now!

The take-off was fun and I was fine as the pilot swooped up into the air and steadied the plane at about 2,000 feet. Then, without warning, he nosed the plane straight over into an outside loop. As we went through the nose-straight-down position into hanging by the seat belt upside down, I started falling out of the plane as the seat, which was not locked down, now went all the way to the top position and somehow got locked. I was now chest high above the wind screen with nothing to hold on to and only being held in by the seat belt. After completing the outside loop and being in the level position for a mere second, he then did a snap roll into a regular loop, all with me flopping around trying to unlock the up position of the seat with arms and upper torso struggling against gravity and wind. The flight wasn't long and I only remember I was too scared to throw up. When we landed, I wobbled over to Johnny who asked excitedly, "You want to go again?" I suggested to John that he do something to himself that is impossible.

Quick Stories about Trains

I still love trains. When I was a very young boy, my mom and my sister and I would take my dad dinner when he was working late at the cannery. If I heard a train whistle, I would run and sit on the concrete floor with my legs hanging out of the loading dock doorway and feel the vibration in the concrete start while the steam locomotives and train were over a mile away. These giant trains came within 20 feet of the door and the noise and vibration were unreal. The steam engines (20 were built by Baldwin) were the largest ever in the world. There were 22 wheels supporting the boiler. They had two sets of 8 drive wheels and were "articulated," which means the under carriages were hinged between the two sets of drive wheels so they could negotiate the curves because of the extreme length of the boiler. The engineer cabs were forward. This kept the smoke out of the engineer's compartment when they went through the many tunnels while struggling up the grade out of Los Angeles through Glendale, Burbank, San Fernando and up the Tehachapi mountains. Because of the steepness of the grade, there would be 2 engines hooked together forward, 2 in the middle and 2 pushing the train of more than 80 freight cars. Upon reaching the top of the grade, 4 of the engines would be pulled out, hooked together and come roaring back down the grade. If they hit anything like a truck or car in San Fernando, they couldn't get stopped until Glendale, some 15 miles later.

I do remember a bad train ride though. I was stuffed on a train by Frank Anderson in Los Angeles with a slight concussion after being dropped on my head in an induction ceremony into the Kappa Sigma fraternity. By the way, I believe I am still the only man in existence to go through "Hell Week" alone. I was bound for Ocala, Florida and spring training which is why I was alone in "Hell Week" as I had to leave school at USC early.

Upon boarding the train, I was more than delighted to see a large group of very nice looking gals, all traveling together, having their bags being put on board. There was also a group of guys with them, but they didn't seem to be interested in the gals, so I was sure that the four-day trip would be a delight. I mean, after all, I showered daily, had a couple of bucks and was not married. I also had a private compartment!

The damn train got a "hot box" (wheel trouble) outside of San Bernardino and now it would take five days to get to Florida. That I could live with, but the girls and guys turned out to be part of a traveling ballet troop and the boys liked the boys and girls liked the girls. How many Readers Digests can a guy read?

IN THE ARMY

Prize Fight in Basic Training

Basic training Army-style was ugly to say the least. I think it lasted 14 weeks which is enough time to love or hate anything. I was left in between because no one can like the brainwashing needed to make a soldier follow a command without a thought of his own safety, but it was my first taste of the fact that there were a lot of guys dumber than I and I reveled in it.

I found that I had a certain respect from a few that could translate into making my life better in that environment. In essence, I thought I could have an impact on all the guys living in the downstairs area of our two-story wooden barracks.

On the upper floor, there was a broad shouldered big guy whose name I think was Peltier with a up-beat personality and I felt, along with everyone up there, that he was the man. Get the picture? He had control of the upstairs and I felt good about my guys below.

All went well until we had a confrontation in the head. It was over some stupid thing concerning the mopping of the place and whose turn it was to do it. I found myself thinking, "Jesus, I hope I don't have to knock this guy down to prove my point," because he kept smiling at everything I said.

Somehow we walked out of there without going that extra minute that we would have regretted because we remained friends for the 14 weeks and as it turned out, I would have regretted more than him because a week later we were marched to a gym to watch some boxing matches. They had a ring set up above the crowd just like at regular fights.

The fights were fun and no one was getting beat up too badly while we were rooting and howling like freed dogs, since this was the first non-Army thing we had a chance to do since arriving at Camp Roberts, California.

The last fight of the evening was terribly different and I was shocked to see Peltier being ushered into the ring after being announced as the dark horse. He was to fight the Camp Roberts heavyweight champion who had held the title for a year or so.

Well it was ugly! He hit the guy so hard with his first punch that every soldier in the audience winced and, if that wasn't enough, he hit the guy on his way down so hard it sent the poor bastard sliding backward under the ropes to wind up hopelessly bent over backwards half hanging over the edge of the platform. I thought the guy was dead. I can't remember to this day two harder punches.

Afterwards and until the end of basic training, our downstairs guys never said a word about cleaning the head. And you can bet I was there helping!

A Bad Night

There has never been a darker night. It was impossible to see the man in front of me within arms' reach and the orders were filtered back to stay in line as we moved up to the base of Hill 222 (the number denotes meters in height). "They must be crazy," I thought as I strained to see anything. "What hill?" I whispered, thinking to myself, "this is madness!"

George Company had been ordered to replace Fox Company whom we had seen in the fading light stumbling down the trail with their dead and wounded. I had spotted a redheaded guy being carried by four guys in a poncho and realized I knew him as a ball player with the St. Louis Cardinal organization that I had played against in the California League; his left leg below the knee wasn't there and he was dying. As we passed them going in different directions, I asked a guy in the other line what it was like. He started to reply and then just put his head down and slowly said, "They overran us. We didn't get all our people off the hill." Then he said as we got further apart, "I hope you make it."

There is no way to tell you in words what the next four hours were like except to say it was brutal chaos. In the blackness, we somehow got to the top of the totally blasted hill and as I went by the lieutenant who led us to the top, he was crying. He later had to be replaced. No wonder, as we had to crawl over unseen dead bodies in a trench that paralleled the mountain top and the blood would erupt when you put an arm down on a corpse to advance forward. In the morning light I used my canteen water to get the blood off my hands and gear, hoping I wouldn't need it later. I shouldn't have wasted it as the dawn brought mortar rounds on us every few seconds for the next 20 terrifying hours. During the unrelenting bombardment, my buddy Bob Souza and I spent the time digging further down into the ground until it took a grenade box placed on end to aid in getting out.

Those hours were made worse because there was a dead GI not five feet away from the foxhole Bob and I were lucky enough to dive into. It is a picture in my mind that I have with me today. He was a good-looking blonde kid, my age, just staring wide eyed to the heavens. Every time I peered out of the foxhole, I was hoping he would wink at me and come to life. He never did. He should have been surfing at Malibu or taking a spring break from college in Fort Lauderdale, but instead he got killed on a war-torn no-name mountain in the middle of Korea.

It is funny how the mind works. Never once, in the four and a half months I spent in combat, did I have the thought that I might wind up the same way.

Adrenaline

A group of us were out of our foxholes sitting in the sun trying to get warm on the back side of Hill 272. It was before noon in Korea in late September of 1951. We had taken some incoming mortar rounds earlier that day and two guys were killed. They were caught out of their foxhole and the first damn round got them both. Some called it a lucky round and some called it fate but, no matter, it was awful. We sat there in the rare warmth cleaning our weapons and talking about the heroism of the medic who went out into the open to try to save the one guy still moving. He worked as hard as he could without even a thought of his own destiny as mortar shells chewed up earth all around him.

Then our attention was diverted to our company Jeep (with trailer) coming hell bent down the road in the valley towards the stream crossing below us. I can still see that Jeep churning up dust and going much faster than designed with four guys holding on for life, including the driver. They were bringing the chow, but believe me, it wasn't their idea. They had been ordered to get the hot food to the front. If it had been left up to them, to a man they would have said, "Let 'em eat dirt" and, really, all of us would have understood.

It was our company's (George CO. 7th Cav. Reg.) policy to get the veterans off the front line and make them cooks when they got close to rotating home. None of the four guys riding in that Jeep wanted any part of revisiting the front. To them it was just tempting the odds. Each one of those men had fifteen months on line! When you think that they were only drafted for 24 months, it is hard to believe the unfairness of some men being relegated to front line combat for that long.

At any rate, the Chinese must have seen the dust rising and, just as the Jeep approached the stream crossing, a Chinese mortar crew started firing at them. The first round hit off to their right and the driver swerved to the left and DAMN, the Jeep got stuck about a third of the way across the stream bed. As the second round hit closer to their left, the three non-drivers leaped from the Jeep and grabbed the sides of it as the driver was trying to put it into four-wheel drive, and threw the whole rig (trailer and all) back onto the solid stream crossing.

From our vantage point it was like watching a Keystone Comedy act and we howled with delight as they sped the rest of the way into the safe area under our hillside position. Then, after the welcome hot meal, six guys went down to see if they could move the parked Jeep and trailer sideways. Not a chance. Adrenaline is a strange and wonderful thing and when fear was added to the equation it created three supermen who, by the way, were sent home the following week.

Top: I'm the tall one standing next to a suspected enemy that was routed out of a burning shed.
Bottom: Finally aboard the troop ship out of hell.

Tennis Shoes

On a black night in the fall of 1951 the 3rd Platoon of George Company, 7th Cavalry Regiment, 1st Cavalry Division was holed up in a waist deep trench along the front side of Hill 222.

We would spend the daylight hours on the back side of the hill in foxholes to get out of the direct line of fire from the Chinese cannons, but there was no place to hide from the constant lobbing mortar fire. Hill 222 is situated where the Imgin-Gang and the Yokkok-Chon rivers meet in the middle of Korea above the 38th parallel.

On moonless nights, the division people in the rear would shine searchlights on clouds over the front lines to silhouette the skyline for us and only a fool would take his helmet off, as it was the only way to identify an enemy. The Chinese had no helmets.

Some time after midnight, maybe later, my foxhole buddy, Bob Souza, was sleeping and I was peering forward when I got a funny feeling something was different. I nudged Souza and turned my head sharply around to the left and in the corner of my eye saw a shape silhouetted maybe twenty feet above us. It moved quietly another couple of feet and hunched down behind a small shattered tree. The shape had no helmet! I jerked the bolt on my M-1 and said, "I'll give you three to say something in American." I started, "one." To my left someone said "shoot the prick" and with that I cut loose. I had seven rounds left in the clip and fired them. Then jammed in another full clip and emptied it. Then silence.

Down the trench the lieutenant yelled "who is firing that BAR (Browning Automatic Rifle)?" Sousa hollered, "We think Sully just killed a gook!" Then my heart sank when the Lieutenant said, "Jesus Christ, I've got a runner out there you stupid sons of bitches! Go check it out and give me an answer fast." The runner was supposed to be moving between positions to tell us to get ready to move off the hill in thirty minutes. "Bob, I'm sure that bastard didn't have a helmet on." "OK Sully, let's do this fast." We both knew that if it was the enemy and he was only wounded, we could both be dead in a minute. To his everlasting credit and my everlasting gratitude, he crawled out of that trench with me. With our rifles ready, we scrambled as fast as we could upward on our hands and knees to the shattered stump in the pitch black, groping with our left hands. We really couldn't see a damn thing and then suddenly Bob said, "I got tennis shoes here." I almost cried with relief; Chinese soldiers didn't have boots either.

Silence

I will go to my grave remembering the silence of the battlefield. Except for the mortal fools who remain on both sides to wreak more havoc and death, nothing is left to make noise. Blasted and torn into shredded stumps, trees, as you know them, are gone. No birds or crickets or animals of any kind except for an occasional rat will disturb the unholy quiet and it will be blown to bits the minute it makes the mistake of creating noise in the empty ration cans thrown down by the barbed wire or in the ravines to warn of the approaching enemy. It's as if it were a jet black page and any bit of sound puts a jagged white line somewhere on it.

Between the clashes of combat that render the ears numb with the ripping, smashing unholy din and the screams of the wounded and dying, the silence is overwhelming. Not wanting to disturb this silence, soldiers sneak around, bent over from place to place as if that will help. Should an empty water canteen be dropped and hit a rock, the echo through the mountains literally stops men in their tracks. They hold their breath and wait and listen. Then if, off in the distance, there is a muffled "thump" the combat soldier knows he has only seconds to get flat before the deadly mortar round will come seeking that canteen and the dunce who dropped it.

There was an afternoon our platoon was assigned the laying of the barbed wire within earshot of the enemy. Each swing of the sledge hammer pounding the stakes into the bare mountain hillside was like ringing a giant bell just begging for trouble. Our rifles were stacked above the wire but short of our mountain top position. Knowing we had to first get back through the wire to safety made it even more stressful. It was swing the sledge hammers and listen for "thumps".

Suddenly, one was heard and it created a mad scramble to get through the wire for our weapons. Realizing we couldn't make it, Bob Souza (my foxhole buddy) and I dove into a small recession in the hillside praying our luck would hold. It did, but two guys from 2nd Platoon were caught at a tree stump where their rifles had been slung by the carry straps. Unbelievably, they were arguing about whose gun was whose when the mortar round hit the very tree stump.

In the horrible silence that ensued, we listened to the two dead bodies tumbling down the mountain side, only to be stopped by the very barbed wire they lost their lives to lay.

The problem with total silence is the memories that put scratches on clean black paper.

Top left: "Man! You're too tall to be in the Army!"
Top right: A chow line is a chow line no matter where you go.
Right: Practicing skiing before an ugly presentation in Japan.

Practice Makes Imperfect

In the dead of winter and on skis, "Surprise Squad in Attack" was to be demonstrated by my squad to George Company. They would be marched out some eight miles from camp using snow shoes and positioned at the bottom of a long sloping hill by our company commander, Lt. Munson. We would be swooping down out of the dense stand of trees that ringed the top of the hill.

We were given three days practice and considering there was no lift to the top, it was fun training for the event. We dressed in our winter clothing and used light jackets or sweaters and stocking caps as we skied down the hill in a pretty "V" with me in the lead. On the third day I pronounced us ready. Ah, the failure of youth to foresee the future...

The day of the demonstration dawned bright and clear in the hills outside of Sapporo and we were taken to the site by snow vehicles the army called "weasels." They were low, open weapon carriers with tracks and could go good in water and snow. In fact, on weekends we skied behind them using ropes just like water skiing. At any rate, we were being transported to the top of the hill because this time we were taking all of our combat gear. Steel helmets, weapons, ammunition, including two bandoliers apiece. Are you starting to see the problem? We didn't!

Lt. Munson, had the troops in position and through a speaker phone called out "Sgt. Sullivan! Begin your attack!"

We came out of the forest perfectly. I looked back and strung out in a perfect "V" on both sides of me were my men spaced just right. I did notice that I was sure going a hell of a lot faster than in training. In fact, I was starting to try to snowplow (slow) the trail skis we were wearing when Jenkins, who was carrying the 30 cal. machine gun, shot by me wide-eyed and lost control. It wasn't a pretty sight and thankfully he managed to toss the heavy gun prior to an ass-over-tea-kettle ending. Unfortunately, he would not be the only casualty of the moment. Williams, who was carrying two boxes of machine gun ammo with his rifle strapped on his back, just gave me a blank stare as he blew past and crashed into a small bush. The unaccounted-for weight was doing us in and, one by one, all my men ate it. There was no conversation or yelling, just the grunt of impact and the crashing of metal on metal echoing through the hills.

I was the last to fall. My steel helmet rolled the rest of the way down the hill and settled exactly in front of Lt. Munson, a combat veteran with the respect of every man I knew. He merely looked at me and without saying a word, turned and marched the troops back to camp. Some days were better than others in Japan.

I would rather not comment on either of these events put forward by the publishers. At least we had ties on.

Rickshaw Racing

I spent 1952 in Japan on the northern most island of Hokkaido. The entire 1st Cavalry Division had been pulled out of Korea and the 7th Cavalry Regiment was assigned to Camp Crawford near the city of Sapporo, population over 600,000.

Memories of that eventful year must start off with our infamous rickshaw races. After a fine Friday night meal at the Sergeant's Club, a number of us would catch the military bus to the bridge that crossed the river into town. There we would each choose our rickshaw for the night and let the races begin! The rickshaws were three-wheeled bicycles with a side-by-side seat for two in the back. Each race was to a predetermined saloon as far across town as we could think of. Last man to arrive at the bar in his chosen rickshaw paid for the round of drinks. Sergeant Stretz was always given a fairly large handicap lead as he was considerably overweight and smaller head starts were dolled out begrudgingly because of various other sporting reasons such as, the rickshaw driver had a bad cough, or the dog chained to the yoke of the bike to help pull had the mange. In the winter the seat was enclosed and had a coffee can with a few charcoals for warmth.

The monetary exchange was 360 yen to the dollar, so prior to each race a bargain had to be struck with the driver of choice, but it was not uncommon as your rickshaw came up even with another competitor, to hear "Faster boysan! 1,000 yen for more speedo."

One very cold winter night, the races were held on frozen streets and all of us had arrived at the finish but Sergeant Stretz and Sergeant Breenan. This particular bar was at the very end of a dead end street. Shortly, we heard them coming and damn if they weren't side-by-side as they came sliding around the corner. You could hear Breenan hollering "I got 3,000 yen here boysan" and Stretz had his canopy open and was simply screaming threats at his poor man.

Then it happened! We saw they could never stop in time. Stretz and Breenan could see it wasn't going to work out. The drivers were standing on their brakes which was useless because of the ice, and before the impact that literally tore off the front of the bar made of bamboo and rice paper I distinctly remember the poor dogs that were now being dragged into the collision, sitting bolt upright sliding on the ice, front legs straight out trying for traction and their eyes as big as full moons. The ensuing crash was total. We took one look at the broken bamboo, pissed off drivers, bent bicycle wheels, barking dogs and the soot from the destroyed pot belly stove and took off in all directions to escape the MPs that were sure to follow. The U.S.Army has no humor and we were to race no more.

Hoops Heaven

Lt. Munson banged open the door and slid two cases of Canadian Club across the floor of the single barracks that housed all of what was left of G company, 7th Cavalry Regiment. "You got no orders for 10 days!" he yelled and left.

This could not be true. None of this could be real. Just days ago we were in hell and now we were in heaven. Just days ago, life was virtually hanging on a thread as we were holed up 30 yards apart, one man to a hole, on 24-hour watch in an active combat area of Yonchon, Korea, praying the Chinese wouldn't know how thinned out we were. And now we were in a steam heated, one-story brick building with beds, pillows, sheets and hot showers. None of which I had seen for four and a half months of existing like a rat. It was December of 1951.

The entire 1st Cavalry Division had been pulled out of Korea, no longer combat fit and the 7th Cavalry Regiment was assigned to Camp Crawford near the city of Sapporo, population more than 600,000 and, of all things, we were paid all our back pay and allowed to go into that city fresh from the front lines.

Most of us just wore ourselves out. How much can you drink? How many kimonos can you chase? About a week into it, I awoke one morning to find the barracks with a lot of guys just sleeping in. I remember later sitting on the steps in front of the barracks with some of the guys, talking and really just getting to know each other, because most of us had been replacements and you don't go around being introduced in combat. By the way, every veteran will tell you being a replacement is the absolute worst way to go into combat, because you haven't got a clue about the man next to you and he isn't happy about being a nursemaid either.

At any rate, the conversation got around to sports and who played what. Turned out that the four guys I was sitting on the steps with were basketball players. Nothing to do but go over to the gym and shoot around a little. In the gym was a team in uniforms and practicing on one of the courts. The five of us shot some baskets and then asked the coach of the uniformed team if he would like to scrimmage with us. He did and we beat the hell out of them in our stockings. It turned out they were the Hokkaido Service Champions.

The regiment scrounged around some old red uniforms and shoes and we became the Red Raiders. With a guy named Beecham from the medics and Ed Bartosik from F Company, along with Alvin Wright and Ken Williams and me from G Company, we went on to win 32 straight games and became all-services champions, beating the paratroopers in the finals at Sendai, Honshu.

Top: I'm number 13, it's the tip-off of the championship game in Sendai, Japan.
Bottom: Lt. Ray Gestaut, our coach, looks on as Major General Thomas Harrold awards the basketball trophy. I accepted on behalf of the team.

Cruising Courtesy of Uncle Sam

The Army has a navy they call Troop Ships. This falsely implies that they are built to carry troops, but as any poor son-of-a-bitch who's ever been on one will tell you, they are built to carry cattle. The ugly truth is 224 men try to sleep in a 30' x 30' room, literally unable to turn over because of the closeness of the man above! As the days go by, the body odor reaches a level that has rats leaping into the sea. If the guy on the top bunk gets seasick....well, it's not good. Meals are served in a huge galley that features no chairs or stools. You stand shoulder to shoulder while eating and pray no one is cursed with "mal-de-mer" once again. Another adventure is a visit to the partition-less "head" when the ship is rolling. For starters the 20' long urinal trough is not designed for waters more violent than a bird bath. So, trust me, sitting on the "John" with the urinal disgorging its contents around your ankles while you try to avoid the eyes of the guy directly across from you and rubbing shoulders with guys on both sides in time with the roll of the ship is, to say the least, distracting! There has never been a shred of modesty left on one single soul disembarking from a 14-day voyage provided by Uncle Sam!

We had been at sea for six days when I finally managed to be third in line at breakfast. A little midget of a lieutenant came by and flipped my shirt button and it came loose, technically making me out of "dress code." Hard to believe a little shit could do that to me and get away with it, isn't it? Well, in the Army they have a set of rules that they easily enforce by insisting you either comply or go to jail forever if an officer so desires! So, this lieutenant says "follow me soldier" and along with five other hand-picked slobs, I trailed along, totally troubled with justice as it was initially explained to me. We were led down flights of stairs to the very bowels of this ship taking 2,500 GIs overseas to Japan. The air was getting more humid and there seemed to be an aroma surrounding what we were coming up on. The lieutenant opened the bulkhead door and barked out, "Give up your dogtags and you'll get them back when this room is sanitized!" There are no words for what we were looking at or what we were smelling. Piled ceiling high, were pots and pans randomly thrown in this quagmire of guck with nary a wipe off from the last six days at sea.

As the little bastard came for my tags I bolted. It was the only time I ever disobeyed an order and, while racing back up those stairs and ignoring his "Stop or I'll shoot" bullshit as I was positive his finger wasn't loaded, I resolved that if worse came to worst I would join hands with the next batch of rats.

Trappist Monastery

I am not Catholic but, when I was asked to go along on a Catholic retreat in 1952 by Lieutenant Ray Gestaut, the coach of the basketball and baseball teams I played with when I was in the service in Japan, I said sure. Anything seemed better than the day to day activities of camp life.

Eight of us went by train to the southern tip of Hokkaido. How does one explain a retreat? Better yet, how does one explain a retreat when at the gate you are told never to speak. No words period! For five days! "They're kidding Lieutenant, right?" "No, Sully, and that also means when we are in our sleep area alone." "Well how the hell are we supposed to know where to go and what to do?" I asked. It was all explained to us by the Abbot (head man) at the lower gate. "Here is the schedule and just listen for the bells." I couldn't believe it, but for the next five days I never said a word. I know, you don't believe it either, right?

The monastery was awesome. It was perched on the very top of a hill and from the gate house we climbed the long straight rutted road to reach the upper gate of the great wall that surrounded the entire inner complex. Before going inside, I looked back and there was the gate house framed by the sea looking south toward the largest of the Japanese islands, Honshu.

Everything, I mean everything, was done in house from scratch. There was no electricity. They made the robes and the belts they wore from the sheep they herded; It was old, stark, foreboding and completely void of any human comforts including plumbing. The monks slept on board beds. We slept on a hardwood floor. We ate plain mutton.

There was an old man there who was sort of second in command. He had been a WWI German pilot. On the last day, he was allowed to talk. It was so strange to him that he kept giggling. He was curious why we wore military clothing. One has to remember that Hokkaido, the northern most Japanese island, was simply ignored in WWII and this German was really not aware of it happening, much less the Korean conflict.

What did I get out of it? One: I could never be a monk. Two: I'll never eat mutton again. Three: Silence is a precious thing to be valued highly and with the denial of human pleasures, there seems to emerge a clearer picture of one's self and the need to be at ease with that image.

Sworn to never speak the rest of their lives except for the chanting of their nightly vespers, the monks spent every waking hour away from their duties praying for the rest of humanity. There are some, I fear, who may not be worth it.

EARLY YEARS IN BASEBALL

Deciding to Sign

A Red Sox baseball scout named Jack Corbett came to the Burbank Recreational Park in California where I was pitching in an American Legion baseball game. He watched the game and called my parents. After he came to the house, it was decided that I should travel with Mr. Corbett to Boston.

My travels, up until then, comprised driving with my father over the Ridge Route in a 1936 Dodge to see my grandmother in Sacramento. We left after he got off work on a Friday afternoon and stopped sometime in the night at a motel, not knowing it was located about 15 feet from the railroad tracks. I'll never forget, in the middle of the night, when that giant steam engine and long line of loaded freight cars, came thundering down the grade. I don't know how we stayed in the bed and it was the only time I ever saw my father "wide-eyed."

I also remember traveling with my family to see Boulder Dam (Hoover now) and we stayed in a motel in Las Vegas when there were only two casinos on the main street.

Now I was to travel across the entire country with someone I hardly knew for a tryout with the Boston Red Sox at Fenway Park.

Mr. Corbett and I were in the lobby of the Somerset Hotel in Kenmore Square, Boston, Massachusetts, and Mr. Corbett introduced me to Maurice McDermott and Chuck Stobbs. They asked me if I'd like to go uptown with them, as the game had been rained out. I couldn't believe it. We took a cab (my first ride in one) to downtown Boston and Washington Street. Maurice directed the driver to the Arrow shirt store and Chuck dispatched him with a tip of five dollars. He actually tipped him five dollars! That was my two-week allowance!

Maurice strode into the store with Chuck, while I absorbed all the stares and gesturing from the people walking by, recognizing the two Red Sox pitching stars.

When I caught up with them in the store, Maurice was saying to the clerk, "I'll take a dozen of these shirts and I'll wear this one." He took off the shirt he was wearing, put on the new shirt and left the shirt he was wearing in the store. Are you kidding? My Dad worked in a cannery. We lived in a house trailer.

Up until then, baseball was something to do when I wasn't playing basketball. I loved basketball and still do. I made the All-California Interscholastic Federation team a couple of years and had a scholarship to Stanford waiting, but take off your shirt and leave it in a store?

That's when I made the decision to sign a pro baseball contract, if it was offered. It was. It remains a perfect example of things not being what they seem.

Top: Fenway in all its glory.
Bottom: My first tryout in Fenway Park; Larry Woodall, Johnny Murphy, Jack Corbett,
George Toporcer and me.

LIFE IS MORE THAN 9 INNINGS

Welcome to Professional Baseball

Jack Corbett, the Red Sox scout I had signed with, drove me to San Jose and left me off at the ballpark. I did not know a soul. I was fresh out of high school. I can remember the wave of fear that swept over me as I joined the club in mid-season.

Somehow I made it to the office and told them my name and was shown the home team locker room. There were a few, much older guys in there putting their uniforms on, but not one of them said a word to me. I had with me a pair of baseball shoes, a glove, a jockstrap and protector. Finally the clubhouse man came over and gave me a uniform, which consisted of uniform pants, uniform shirt, uniform socks and a cap. I didn't know I was to furnish the belt, undershirt and inside white stockings (sanitary socks). He saw me fumbling around half dressed and came over with the missing items which he said I was to pay for. I told him I didn't have enough money with me and he said not to worry, he would get it out of my paycheck. Remarkably, players in my era had to supply the sanitary socks and sweatshirts and underwear which we bought by the dozen. Also, the jockstraps, protectors, baseball gloves and baseball shoes.

I had never worn sanitary socks. I didn't know they existed. I have to tell you, that all my baseball life, I felt I was betraying manliness when I put on those white cotton hose. They were rather sheer and long enough to come up over my knees. I watched how the other players pulled them up over their knees and then pulled the outside socks up over their knees and either taped or put a rubber band above the calf of their leg, then rolled them down together. I had always worn regular sweat socks under the outside socks, so the sanitary socks felt really different, but I was proud of the way they looked. I went out through the tunnel into the back of the dugout and sat down. Batting practice was underway for our team.

The oldest man in uniform saw me and came over. He was the manager of the San Jose Red Sox of the Class C California League. His name was Marv Owen and he had been a third baseman for the Detroit Tigers and a teammate of Ty Cobb. He said, "I want you to throw batting practice in fifteen minutes. I'll call you when it's time to warm up."

Two of the older players came over and sat on each side of me, without saying a word they looked me straight in the eye, turned, and spit slimy tobacco juice down on my brand new sanitary socks! I saw Marv Owen watching and smiling.

Welcome to professional baseball in the summer of 1948.

Opposite: A picture of me right out of high school when I joined the San Jose Red Sox.

Hitting Signs for Money

In 1949, Pinky Higgins, before he became manager of the Boston Red Sox, was managing the Birmingham Barons of the Southern Association. Of all things, he was having a hard time winning games with a good team because of a downtown store promotion. Black's Department Store was offering a pair of slacks to any Baron who hit a double, a sport coat for any Baron who hit a triple and a suit for any Baron who hit a home run.

I'm here to tell you it was comical! No one was stopping at first base if they hit the ball fair. Players were being thrown out at second base by sixty feet! I remember Cal Burlingame, our center fielder, streaking for third after barely reaching second base safely by one step, only to be tagged out by the third baseman who damn near fell asleep waiting for him to get there.

When Pinky screamed at Cal about it, Bob DiPietro took it upon himself to defend Cal by shouting, "Hell, Pinky, you know how bad that coat he's got now is!" Pinky's reply only seemed to extend the problem when he said, "Yeah, most people burn something that old and ugly."

Back then, in the minor leagues, there always seemed to be an outfield fence sign to hit and get something. Like a set of four tires or a battery for the car or a week's free pass to the drive-in movie or a free lunch, etc. Of course the pitchers who didn't get to play every day always felt slighted. Make that cheated.

Then, can you imagine my dismay when there were no signs or anything to aim at when I got to the major leagues? Where was the bull's-eye? Where was the extra reward? Not even a pair of slacks or a free lunch!

My first major league contract was for $6,000 which meant I was losing money playing the game. There were the food bills and rental houses in spring training and in Boston. There were the auto expenses along with the tipping in all the baseball clubhouses and the purchasing of the baseball shoes and gloves and wool undershirts not to mention the $4.00 a day meal money given to us on the road trips that had to be added to. (Beer wasn't free then either.)

So when you're compelled to look up my lifetime batting average and realize it was somewhat limp, I can only tell you I tried to stay as motivated as possible without having an extra reward while facing Early Wynn, Bob Feller, Bob Lemon, Herb Score, Bob Turley, Jim Bunning, Frank Lary, Mike Garcia, Ryne Duren and a host of other hard throwing, mean, angry, unpredictable, knock-down artists.

OK! OK! I'll be honest with you. Most of the time I went to bat against those guys trying not to cry out, "I want my mommy!"

Water Bombing

When youth is subjected to boredom it can, at times, bring out the worst in behavior. Which brings to mind a bad afternoon in Utica, New York, while playing baseball for the Albany Senators of the Class A Eastern League.

My roommate, Jake Donaldson, and I were hanging around in our hotel room with about four hours to kill. We spotted a bright red Chevy convertible with four girls in it that kept coming around the block. When they had to stop at the red light, we were ready and let go two wastepaper baskets full of water. The problem was Jake's basket slipped from his hand and went with the water from 13 floors up. Luckily, the light turned green and the car went forward and avoided a disaster. Then panic took over as we spotted a policeman on the corner looking up and pointing. We had to move quickly to get another basket. After knocking on the door across the hall and getting no answer, I put Jake on my shoulders and he went through the transom window above the door into the room and got a basket. He came out the door and we were just back in the room when the authorities arrived. Finding two indignant guys playing cards and with the right amount of wastepaper baskets in the room, they reluctantly moved on down the hall. Whew!

Looking back now on 14 years of water activity, it is my belief that the all-time event was pulled off in the Lord Baltimore Hotel in Baltimore, Maryland, when I was with the Red Sox. Sam White and I had been thinking for two years about a new and more accurate and powerful water bombing. We called it the "Waterfall."

The Shriners were in town and, believe me, there was no sleep for anyone in any mid-town city when they or the American Legion were having a convention. For one thing, they had a big bell mounted on a four wheel trailer. It was parked next to their favorite entrance and exit to the hotel on a side street under the Red Sox rooms, which were lined up nicely in a row on the 11th floor. The damn bell was manned constantly by idiots who took turns beating on it with anything they could find. When it got dark, they seemed to find bigger bell bangers.

The bell ringing was unrelenting when we got back to the hotel after the game and dinner. It was time! Even teammates who were disinterested in our efforts in the past found reason to join this crusade. We had nine rooms ready with two wastepaper baskets of water and on a given signal "WATERFALL!"

It was beautiful and after five more waterfalls, the street looked like the Mississippi River and the bell was moved to the other side of the hotel by Shriners in raincoats to the cheers of our teammates. As White and I entered the clubhouse the next day, we were accorded a standing ovation. Life, at times, can be so sweet.

Riding Buses

In 1948, after failing an incredible amount of times to throw the ball into the strike zone to see what might happen, I was sent from the San Jose Red Sox (Class C) of the California League to the Oroville Red Sox (Class D) of the Far West League. I met the team in Pittsburg, California, and was immediately told to throw my gear on the bus as they were leaving. The bus was a straight-back-seat yellow school bus that the club had rented because their own bus had broken down. The players' luggage was piled in the aisle and had to be crawled over to get to a seat because the bus was a day-timer with no outside space for travel bags. The only seat left for me was on the four bags of bats thrown in the back row. The trip was from Pittsburg to Klamath Falls, OR, a distance of about 335 miles! And get this! The bus had a governor on the motor that wouldn't allow it over 45 mph.

I remember we stopped in Weed, California, at 2 AM for gas and a bite to eat in a restaurant that, I kid you not, had a single totally exposed light bulb swinging on a wire in the middle of the room! (I think I ate standing up to get the blood back into my bat-bag sitting butt.)

Strangely, our bus driver was the second baseman because I was told our manager and trainer/driver had gone by car to get to the Klamath Falls whorehouse first. Hello?

Ah, the bus rides. So many memories. Sleeping in the upper baggage racks or on the aisle floor; buying a box of 22 rifle shells so you could have a turn shooting out of the window on those lonely roads in the West at night; preferred seats up front if you were having a good year; making a rookie buy beer and try to sneak it on the bus past the manager, which almost always meant the rookie would miss the meal at the way stop. I learned to open the emergency exit door just as we stopped; the ragging on a new driver of any bus with the usual result of a stop and hearing what the driver thought of us amid our applause and laughter.

Which reminds me, when I was with the Phillies we were put on a bus to go to Chicago from Milwaukee. The driver was unaware that he had just loaded on the biggest group of critics of his career, but when he missed Chicago he knew it in spades! I remember I was sitting with Turk Ferrell and he said to me, as we went by a horse racetrack on the outskirts of that huge city, "I'm telling you, Sully, we are now going south of the city." It was true! We had missed Chicago! If you look in your atlas you can plainly see that Milwaukee and Chicago are not only pretty close, they are on the same lake and all you have to do is drive southeast and keep the lake on your left. You can't miss Chicago. You can't! We did! It absolutely mirrored the season we were having and we told the driver he belonged with us.

Top: One of my teammates takes a swing at the ball painted on the back of the Scranton, Pennsylvania Red Sox bus.
Bottom: When I played in American Legion ball I could hit!

Playing Without a Ball

I swear that what you are about to read is true. I also understand that you won't want to believe it and, for that matter, I could hardly believe it either as it developed.

It was 1953 and I was playing ball for the Ciudad Obregon team in the Western League of Mexico. It was my habit, even when I played in the major leagues, during batting practice to hang around third base or shortstop and field ground balls. I knew my managers didn't like it but I felt it was good for two reasons. 1) It kept me alert and active to fielding ground balls. 2) It showed my infielders I was aware of their positions.

Back to the story. It was during batting practice in Obregon and I was at the shortstop position when one of our guys swung and missed, but being the ham I am I fielded the imaginary ball and threw it to first where Hererra, our first baseman, pretended to catch it. There was a murmur in the pre-game crowd.

Next time there was a miss, I did it again and there was applause. Our second baseman looked over at me and nodded. Next time there was a miss hit, I fielded the imaginary ball and whipped it to second and he relayed it to first and the crowd let out a whoop!

As the stands filled, more of our players got into the act when batting practice stopped and we just kept acting out different baseball scenarios. The crowd was now roaring with every successful act and when I started a triple play the fans went nuts!

All of this was fun and inventive, but when an excited fan from the right field bleachers lit a railroad flare and ran across the outfield and threw it into the left field bleachers, I knew we were now treading on thin ice (a rarity in that backward area then). That flare landed about 15 rows up on some señorita's lap and it's a good thing she had on some kind of heavy skirt or she would have gone up in flames. The guy sitting next to her grabbed the thing and immediately ran it down and crossed the field and threw it back up into the stands where it came from.

By that time, we on the field had retreated to our dugout and I was wondering where to cower as this thing was getting out of hand big time. There were more flares being lit and people running and throwing them up in the stands.

Then, like in a bad cowboy movie, the local lawman came down on the field, pulled out his six shooter and fired it into the air five times. It had a great effect! Just as that happened Clint Courtney (our manager), came by me and said, "I'll bet he is saving that last bullet for the fool who started this."

My Adoration of Joe D

In my lifetime there were two Joe Ds and both were from San Francisco. Joe DiMaggio is in the Hall of Fame, but Joe DeMaestri is my idol.

I met the latter in 1948. I was just out of high school when I turned professional and joined the San Jose Red Sox where Joe was the shortstop. I was homesick the minute I got there. I never imagined how alone a kid could feel in a crowd. Joe was the only guy on that team who cared. That first night away from home he helped me get a room in a boarding house out in the Lincoln Park suburb where he was staying. He did it because (my belief) his father, Sil, a wonderful man, would have been disappointed if he hadn't had compassion for a stranger.

Sil, whenever he came to see Joe, would try his best to pump me full of enough confidence to throw the baseball over home plate, but the cause was hopeless. I was listening to coaches telling me how I should throw the ball, not where to throw it my way. Be that what it may, whenever I saw Joe, I hung around him like a pet dog.

In places like Daytona Beach, when we were spring training with the Birmingham Barons in Ocala and a bunch of us chipped in a couple of bucks to let Norm Zauchin (Red Sox first baseman-to-be) bowl because he was as good or better than many professional bowlers in those days and for every game over 220 or something, he'd receive a free ticket to the miniature golf course on the top of the building. Charley Maxwell, Bob DiPietro, Joe and I played free up there for hours.

Joe was traded out of the Red Sox organization and played for the Athletics in Philadelphia and I always nodded at him when he came to the batters' box to face me. I knew he didn't like it because Joe competed as hard as any guy I ever knew and wasn't about to let the moment get sentimental, but later in our careers, I remember a time I was pitching against the Kansas City Athletics after Joe had been traded there from the Yankees. When he came to the plate I smiled at him and he stepped out of the box, put his head down and we both had a great laugh.

I have to tell you, though, the biggest laugh was with Les Eichhorn (Joe's neighbor in San Rafael) here on Kauai. Joe, Les and I were walking on the reef in 3' of water off Anini Beach fly fishing about 75 yards out when Joe spotted a white eel. I can only tell you that the wake he made by his mad dash for safety knocked children down on the shoreline. When Les and I queried him later he said the eel was coiled like a cobra and ready to strike.

Joe, eels don't coil, but you are still my hero.

Castro on the Pier

Growing up in Southern California in the '30s and '40s put me in contact with Mexican kids in my neighborhood, in my schools and in my heart. So in 1949 while pitching with the San Jose Red Sox of the Class C California League, I was delighted to be paired on the rooming list with Sam Castro. He was good looking with a smile that just plain knocked the socks off the ladies he favored.

Sam was a pitcher and a good one, but was too old to be considered a big league prospect. So, to bolster the pitching staff, he had been signed by the San Jose club and was their property, not the Red Sox organization.

We were on the road playing in Ventura, California against the Yankee farm club. The ballpark was close to town, down by the ocean and not far from the long fishing pier that extended well out into the water. After a night game (almost all minor league games were), we were in our room and as Sam put on his solid blue sports jacket, he confided in me that he had a date with a little señorita down at the pier and for me to leave the room unlocked when I turned in. It wasn't a problem for me, but I asked him how he was going to get by manager Marv Owen, who always stationed himself in the lobby until curfew time, checking everyone in. (In the minor leagues, curfew was normally set at just enough time for a guy to ride the bus back to the hotel, eat there or close by and that's all, period.)

We were on the 4th floor which scratched the rope ladder even if we had one (they were too scary above mezzanine height). Was he going to use the fire escape and risk the last 12 feet of the ladder being in the "up" position when he returned?

"No," he said, "I pitched good tonight and I'm the oldest guy. I think Marv will let me go down to the drug store for a cup of coffee because I can't sleep."

It worked, and Marv (like most managers who liked to reward a player) told Sam he would give him an extra hour but not to go anywhere else.

Marv always had trouble sleeping and was in the lobby when Sam came back. Sam waved at Marv and said "Thanks skipper, I should be able to get some sleep now." Marv waved back and said "Goodnight Sam." Then, as Sam passed by Marv and stood at the elevator, Marv said, "and by the way Sam, that trip to the pier will cost you $75.00!"

Castro was so mad when he got to the room that I asked him what was the matter. "I can't believe it. How the hell did that goddamn gringo know where the hell I went?" I had to laugh which made him madder. "Amigo," I said, "anyone would know where you went with all that seagull crap on the back of your coat."

Burlingame Fishes for Balls

In the spring of 1949 I walked into the lobby of the Highlands Hotel just outside of Ocala, Florida, after a five-day train ride from Los Angeles. Johnny Murphy (head of the minor league system for the Red Sox) stood up from a meeting in the spacious room and said, "What the hell are you doing here?"

I produced the letter I had received from him that said my contract had been returned to the Birmingham Barons and spring training would start at such and such a date which was then the next day. What I didn't say was, "Yes I had received another letter only one day prior to my leaving home that said for me to report to Porterville, California for spring training with the San Jose Red Sox of the California League which was to start almost a month later."

When I got that second letter I had already paid for the trip to Florida (to be reimbursed by the ball club) and told all my friends that I was going to spring train there. So I asked my mom (if anyone ever asked) to say I didn't receive the letter before I left. She gave me a deadly look but said she thought it might better their timing in the future. At any rate, Murphy said, "OK, you might just as well stay here until we break camp." Paint a Cheshire cat smile on my mug.

So with no pressure to make the club, I had a hell of a good training camp and learned I was a lousy pinochle player. I even went to Birmingham with the club and pitched in a Southern Association League game before going back out west to Porterville and the San Jose team.

The hotel was perched on some high ground and was surrounded by a golf course. In the evening, Cal Burlingame and I would go down the 100 yards or so to a swamp-like pond that would produce golf balls by the dozen if you didn't mind taking off your pants and wading around the knee high water in your shorts, feeling with your bare feet for the balls. After gathering some, we would go back up to the hotel and have our own driving range action while waiting for dinner.

All went well for the first week or so until one fateful late afternoon. Cal was wading about 10 feet in front of me more to the middle of the pond when I heard him gasp! I mean he sucked in enough air to make him 10 pounds lighter in water! "What's wrong?" I said. "What's wrong? Take a look at those two eyes!" Cal blurted out and as I caught sight of the alligator, Cal almost ran right over the top of me getting out of that pond.

At least I had the decency to stop and put on my pants before running back up to the hotel. Cal didn't. I remember there was a memo that went out the next day about a dress code that was in effect for all the ball players housed there.

Getting to the Major Leagues

The last team I played for in the minor leagues before being drafted into the Army was Scranton, Pennsylvania, in 1949. I didn't pitch well and developed a very sore shoulder. The former great relief pitcher for the Yankees and head of the Red Sox farm system then, Johnny Murphy, was working for the Red Sox and sent me along with fellow pitcher Joe Reedy to Avalon Beach on the New Jersey coast to see his favorite rub man. I do not remember that miserable bastard's name and, in fact, I don't care to, but I will always remember the pain. The man was brutal. Joe and I would delay seeing each other after we got rubbed because we wanted the tears to dry. At any rate, as I went into the service, I was unaware that I was designated "NO PROSPECT" by the organization.

In Korea, when my company commander found out I could throw an air burst with a grenade (keep it in the air for more than three seconds so it would explode above the ground) they put me in position to throw at night into hard-to-cover areas. I threw cases of them night after night. Unexplainably, my arm came back!

After spring training of 1953, which I spent with Louisville in Deland, Florida, I was assigned to Albany, New York. Jack Burns was the manager and I wasn't getting to pitch so I went into his office and he leveled with me. "The organization wants me to pitch the "PROSPECTS." I told him my arm was good and asked him to give me a shot anyway he could. He said maybe he could put me into relief some night.

True to his word he did and with the help of Len Okrie, the catcher, I responded. Len called time out in a game at Wilkes-Barre, Pennsylvania. He came out to the mound and said "Sully, you have got to stop worrying about what you are doing out here on the mound and put all your concentration where I am at the plate." Well, it was as if a light went on, and from that moment on I was a totally different pitcher. Soon I was the main relief man and then Jack got very sick. He was in bad shape and went home to Boston to recuperate.

As he got better, he started going to Fenway Park and watching some games. Joe Cronin was the general manager of the Red Sox then and after one particular bad game, Jack was sitting in Joe's office when Lou Boudreau (the team manager at that time) came storming in and asked Joe in a very loud voice, "Haven't you got anyone in this organization that can get the ball over the plate?" "I do," Jack said.

The next night I pitched for the Boston Red Sox and stayed there eight years.

This picture was taken prior to my first starting assignment in the major leagues by a photographer who knocked on my hotel door and said he was there to take a shot of the starting pitcher for the Red Sox that night. I told him he must have the wrong room. He said, "Your name Sullivan?" I nodded and he said, "Well kid, you better get ready because you're it against the Yankees tonight."

No one on the team ever called me.

It was raining in New York that morning so he asked me to sit by the window and look out. I did while trying to stifle the adrenaline rush and I think the caption was something about hoping the rain would end before game time.

The result was my first starting victory (6-3).

IN THE BIG LEAGUES

My First Major League Pitch

I was summoned to the office of the Albany Senators of the Class A Eastern League in August 1953. Classified as a non-prospect, I sat shocked as they said, "You've been called up to the Red Sox. They want you there tonight for tomorrow's game." I remained stunned when the plane landed at Logan Airport and wide-eyed as the cab went into the tunnel under the harbor to Boston.

After a night of fitful sleep in the Kenmore Hotel, I walked into the clubhouse in a daze and saw my name above a locker. Lou Boudreau, the manager, came by as I was putting on the #18 uniform and said, "Can you pitch today if I need you?" I said, "Sure." That's all he said to me. He didn't shake my hand or say hello or anything. Jesus! he wouldn't pitch me today would he? I had just arrived!

It seemed the game against Detroit had barely started and I was still being introduced to the guys in the bullpen when someone said, "Whose sign is that?" From the dugout coach Paul Schreiber was standing on the top step tapping his cap with his right hand. Holy Christ! It was my signal to warm up!

First pitch I threw in the bullpen missed the catcher and slammed into the concrete wall and ricocheted up into the stands. Blood was literally trying to get through my skin. I kept throwing. "If this is a dream you better wake up now fool because they are signaling for you." Someone opened the bullpen gate and I grabbed my jacket, walked onto the field and there was no feeling in my knees.

Then, someway, somehow, I started gathering myself. "Shake yourself Frank, this is the moment!" The bat boy met me in right field and took my jacket without a word. For the first time I sensed the crowd of 20,000 murmuring about a new rookie. "Ignore them dammit, you have got to get control of this. The future is now!" I stopped short of the infield and untied and retied my shoes giving myself just a bit more time to get more positive. It helped and when I reached the mound, I could at least breathe. The umpire was there with Sam White, the catcher, and said, "Took your sweet time getting in here rookie!" I said, "Yeah, but I'm so damn nervous I can hardly walk." "Don't worry kid," the umpire said, "you just get the ball close and I'll call them out." Sam White gave him a quick look then turned to me and said, "Just throw to the glove." They left the mound and I was alone.

The ballpark got quiet as everyone, including me, waited to see what would happen. I took a deep breath and threw the batter a sizzling fastball right down the heart of the plate into Sam's mitt. The crowd cheered. I had done it! The umpire stared at me and called BALL ONE.

The men in blue are another story.

Top: Williams hitting a home run.
Bottom: Jimmy Piersall, Grady Hatton, myself, Sam White and Ted Williams asked to sit for
a winning game photo.

The photo of me and my best friend on the team, Sam White, was taken by some guy wandering around the Sarasota spring training locker room and neither of us were aware of his existence.

I damn near choke up every time I look at this photo because we were buddies doing the very thing we wanted to do and having a fabulous time doing it. Sam was by far the best receiver in the league and his relentless drive to win a game made it impossible for me to back down. We competed as a duo as good as there was for the years the Red Sox allowed us to do our act. I was never as good without him behind the plate.

Sam and I Talking Serious

Sammy White, Boston Red Sox catcher; All-American basketball player at the University of Washington and elected to the school's Hall of Fame for both baseball and basketball; drafted by the Minneapolis Lakers of the NBA; true Bohemian and the most interesting, unpredictable character I will ever know.

I joined the Red Sox in August of 1953 and met the team in Boston where I was somewhat successful, due in large part to Sam. I had never thrown to someone with that much grace and agility behind the plate. He was six feet, three inches tall and could make himself into a two-foot high, one foot wide block that made the catcher's mitt look like a barn door. He could catch a ball with his palm, heel down, no more than two inches off the ground. Umpires might call it a strike as they figured no ball that low could be caught that way. Casey Stengel used to holler to the umpires, "get that reptile off his belly!" Sam also had a burning desire to win and anything less was totally unacceptable.

The first road trip I went on was to Philadelphia to play the Athletics. The team traveled down from Boston by train and arrived in the early evening. We were staying at the Warwick Hotel. In those days, travel days were almost always followed by days off and this was the case, thank God.

While on the train, Tom Dowd, the traveling secretary for the team, gave me a rooming list and I was to room with Sam. We got the key and went to the room and while unpacking, Sam said, "It's my birthday and no one gives a damn! No one has called or left a message or anything. I'm going out to get us two friends!" And out the door he went.

Hey, I better shower and shave, right?" So I did, with great expectations. I put on a little underarm stuff and after-shave lotion. I got a clean shirt out of my bag.

I answered the knock at the door and there was Sam carrying a package. I had wasted the last twenty minutes. In the package were two bottles of Canadian Club. I don't drink Canadian Club to this day because of that night. In fact, we sat in the room and drank both bottles dry and talked of everything there was to talk about. I am not sure when the night ended. I am not sure we ever agreed or disagreed. I don't remember what religion Sam was. The last thing I remember him saying was, "I think we may be together for a long time, so let's never talk about this crap again."

We never did! In the next eight years, we never had a serious conversation. I awoke the next morning with one shoe still on.

Gringos in the Mexican League

In 1953, after my first Major League baseball season was over, I was in my hometown of Burbank, California. A man named Anderson called and said if I would pitch on Sundays for the Rosabell Plumbers (semi-pro team) he would get me a job at the movie studios as a "grip." Damn right I would! I went to work at four in the afternoon, worked till six o'clock on straight time and then got time and a half until quitting time at eleven. We put up and took down sets for TV shows and movies. Every Friday we did the Loretta Young Show. I really enjoyed it and the money was very good at $4.75 an hour.

Then Jack Corbett, the Red Sox scout who had signed me, called and said they were looking for a pitcher down in Mexico and were paying $1,300 a month. Oh? Really? So I drove down to Obregon on the west coast of that country and the headlines read: OTRO BIG-LEAGUER A LA COSTA and SULLIVAN SE UNIO A LOS YAQUIS, which means another beer drinker has arrived.

I joined Don Larsen, Buddy Peterson, Al Heist and Clint Courtney, the other "gringos" on the team, and was put up with them in a two story hotel (no elevator) that had a very high surrounding wall topped off with broken glass. (Good enough hint for me!) Every bit of flooring in that hotel was ceramic tile and after every game, Peterson wasted no time heading for the bar with his baseball spikes on. He was OK going in, but coming out was another story. We never understood why he didn't take his spikes off, but he never did. Later, you could hear him all over the complex. "ROSE! (his wife) ROSE! That's right ROSE! It's me and I'm drunk again. Unlock the goddamn door now Rose, I'm on my way up!" And with that, he would start his skating, falling, sliding, ricocheting, crawling act trying to get to Rose with those damn spikes on. The stairs were difficult for him. When we had nothing to do we would go watch that part of the journey and heckel.

There were no paved roads except for the one main highway through town and there were other problems. No pure water, no cured meat, no pasteurized milk and USA canned foods were scarce. I hate to be this vivid but it was the shits! In fact, in the seventh inning of a game at the town of Navojoa, Clint Courtney had a problem rounding third base and to top it off, he had to slide at home plate.

Even though Clint was the playing manager of the team, we asked him to sit in the back of the bus with all the windows open, alone, as we returned to Ciudad Obregon still in our uniforms. He sat back there puffing on a cigar and, trust me, never was cigar smoke more welcomed. Clint was smiling. We had won the game.

Topcoat in Style

1953, the year the Red Sox called me up, was the last year Boston had two major league teams. In 1954 the Boston Braves became the Milwaukee Braves, and the Red Sox went to play them in a "spring training exhibition game" in that northern city. We were slated for a ticker tape parade on our way to the ballpark. Spring in Milwaukee? I knew what I had to do. I rushed to a downtown store and bought a topcoat with liner. It was a good looking wool tweed topcoat with raglan sleeves in many shades of brown.

The parade went superbly for me as I sat, warm as toast, atop the back seat of a red convertible waving and pointing at good-looking girls and smiling their way. I was a rookie and no one had a clue who I was, but I was having a ball, while my pals were turning blue.

Later, near the end of my baseball career when I was traded to the Phillies, my dressing experience was not as comfortable. It was as if I had been sent back to the Minors because the conditions in Philly in those day were ridiculous. If your locker was under the whirlpool that was situated immediately above on the mezzanine in that awful clubhouse (and mine was), you went home in wet clothes.

I managed to keep my topcoat out of the water, and it served me well for many years. But fashions change, and fifteen years later I said to my wife, Marilyn, while on our way to Las Vegas via my parents' home in Southern California, "I think it's time for me to get a new coat." She didn't think I needed to but agreed to go with me out to North Hollywood where "Oscar Chaum's" men's store was famous for keeping the tall men up to date in fashion.

It was just as I had remembered it when I was in college. I was wearing my old topcoat as we entered. Suddenly a salesman rushed toward me and said, "Wherever did you get that beautiful garment?" I looked over my shoulder wondering who the hell he was talking to. "My God man, it's gorgeous," he said looking up at me straight in the eye. "I haven't seen anything that nice in years." Then he asked, "What can I show you?" I told him about the coat and he said, "Well, sir, you have kept it so long it's back in style."

It was embarrassing the way Marilyn was laughing as I sheepishly walked out of there.

Dinner Lessons from Hoot

In spring training of 1954, Walter "Hoot" Evers demanded that I go to dinner with him in St. Petersburg, Florida, after an exhibition game against the Yankees in which I did well. Evers was the left fielder in 1953 when I joined the Red Sox. He was nine years older than I and always solemn and stern. He had been "around the block" and was close to the end of his baseball career. To be honest, I was not looking forward to the meal but when a veteran said GO, in those days, you went!

Once in the restaurant and seated, he started by saying, "I don't give a damn about what you did in high school. I don't want to know a flaming thing about your combat experience and I sure as hell don't want you to tell me anything you know about baseball. You're too young to know a $%#&* thing about politics and if you once mention the cost of this dinner, I will leave! Understand?" "Yeah, sure Hoot," I stammered. He continued, "Dinner should be eaten with friends. Tales are to be told, not messages to be learned. Dinner is what you get for making it through the day intact and, in essence, should be an easy, relaxing celebration. Understand?" I can't tell you how uncomfortable I was, so I said, "Damn Hoot! Give me a break! I haven't even had the opportunity to read your manual."

Then to my surprise, he smiled and said, "You hungry?" I smiled back and said, "I sure the hell am!" Thinking I was now in calmer waters, I relaxed until he started by ordering chopped liver as an appetizer. The closest I had ever been to liver in my life was when my mom would cook it for the cat and she wore a mask!

Well, it turned out to be one of the most enjoyable meals of my life. This guy was the master of making a dinner meal so interesting that I ate whatever was served without thinking about it and found it all to be great. Dining was his hobby! He planned each evening meal all day long and said it was the thing that kept the boredom of the game from eating him up (his pun not mine). He said he thought I might be in the big leagues for quite a while and I should use the opportunity to explore all kinds of food from the different cities and ethnic groups. As the years went by, I always thought of Hoot when I sampled something new. Like Polish sausage in the west side of Chicago or Hungarian goulash in Manhattan or a boiled dinner in New England or lake crab in Cleveland or oysters and clams and crab out of the Chesapeake in Baltimore. It got out of hand one night in Vermont when I ate black bear meat at a dinner Sam White and I attended for Little League. Afterwards, I felt like chasing cars.

Hoot was dead right about another thing when he said, "The people you eat with have as much to do with the meal as the food."

Top: Leo Kiely, me and Frank Bowman in Sarasota.
Bottom: Frank Malzone, Eddie Mathews (Braves), me, Mickey Vernon (Braves), Sam White and Del Crandall (Braves) before a Jimmy Fund charity game in Boston.

Sam's Evening Diversion

In 1954 the Red Sox were playing a four game series in Philadelphia and I was rooming with Sam White in the Warwick Hotel. After the second game, we were at the bar in a restaurant around the corner from the hotel. The game had been ours but the Athletics pitcher, Amie Portocarrero, was tough and Sam went hitless. I knew he was looking for something to get his mind off the game and when he spotted four limp-wristed guys coming into the establishment, he whirled around on his bar stool and stared at them like a treed raccoon as they went into the dining section. Knowing Sam, I just shook my head as I knew these "guys" would be his diversion for the evening and he would confront them before he left the place. My suggestion that we go somewhere else to eat after another beer was a waste of time. Sam was just itching to chat with these "fellows." Don't get me wrong here; White was a lot of things, but queer wasn't one of them. He also was not a macho idiot jock looking for a fight. On the other hand, I guarantee you, he kept things interesting, to say the least.

We finished our beers and moved into the dining area where we were seated (just my luck) in a booth across from the "boys." The two of us must have stirred something in their souls as there were some blatant stares coming our way. Therefore, I flinched visibly when I caught Sam winking back at one of them.

When dinner was over, nothing else would delay the inevitable. Not wanting any part of it, I simply got up and left for the hotel as Sam pulled a chair up at the outside end of their booth and said, "Hi fellows, I'm a sports writer with the Boston Red Sox. Surely we have something in common?" Knowing how Sam felt about sports writers I felt he had just said it all.

I got back to the hotel and bought a paper and went up to our room. Sam came in about forty-five minutes later. I said, "Well, what did your buddies have to say for themselves?" He said, "I found out I am really wanted somewhere."

Next morning, going to breakfast, we checked the mail box at the front desk as usual. There was a package addressed to Sam White, beautifully hand written in English script. One of those "guys" had sent Sam a pair of expensive white silk boxer shorts. Hand painted on the fly was a flame coming out. Painted on the hip was a naked fireman with a helmet and a fire hose trying to put the fire out. If any other heterosexual in America had received these, they would have trashed the package in secret, not wanting any rumors to start. Sam couldn't wait to put them on in the clubhouse and prance around. He caught six games with them on! I asked him why he didn't wear them for the seventh.

He said the fire had gone out.

How Could it Happen?

When I was informed that my Red Sox teammate had died, I was stunned to the core. Surely it was a bad joke! But it wasn't. It had happened! It was enough to make grown men cry and we did, when Harry Agganis died in June of the 1955 Major League Baseball season.

Maybe the most revered athlete in New England sports history had just passed away from complications following pneumonia. Here was a young man who had it all, knew it and didn't abuse it or waver from his path to exceed.

I was Harry's roommate in the Muelbach Hotel in Kansas City and the night before they sent him back to Boston for treatment had been nightmarish because Harry's cough was, even then, like a death rattle. When we got up the next morning he was gaunt and he said, with a slight smile, that he felt like he looked. I thought to myself that if he felt that bad he was in big trouble. But the thought of a 26-year-old celebrated athlete dying was not thinkable, at least by me.

He was the model for a hero and especially a local one. He was already a legend in his home town of Lynn, Massachusetts, because at the high school level he excelled like no other. Then, as the quarterback for Boston University, he kept up an unbelievable penchant of last-minute winning heroics against big time schools. He played both offense and defense.

All of his Red Sox teammates were aware that this guy was special and was in the blooming process of becoming a fixture at the Major League level without a limit to what could be accomplished. For starters, the guy didn't have an enemy even when he got to the professional level because of the way he handled each person he met. He was a good looking Greek with a lot of elan and savvy. He was becoming one of the best first basemen in the American League. Two days before he died he had raised his batting average above .300. He had the world by the butt and deserved it. There was simply no way he would die. He did! Stunned? Not since my combat tour of Korea had anything been that grim.

Joe Cronin (general manager), Pinky Higgins (manager) and I represented the Red Sox team (playing in Washington, D.C. at the time) at Harry's funeral in Lynn. It was a blistering, cloudless day and we sat in the stifling hot church while thousands walked by his open casket and hundreds bowed and kissed him. I was emotionally overwhelmed by the number of grown men standing on the curbs of Lynn openly crying as our funeral procession passed on the way to the cemetery.

It remains one of the toughest days I have spent on this earth.

1955 All-Star Game and Gene Conley

I was selected to two American League All-Star teams. The first was in Milwaukee in 1955, and by the time Yogi Berra went to the plate in the top of the first, it was already 4-0, with Harvey Kuenn, Nellie Fox, Ted Williams and clean-up man Mickey Mantle (3-run homer) showing why they were all-stars. It was a rocky start for Robin Roberts, who then settled down and pitched two scoreless innings.

Whitey Ford started the 7th for us up 5-0, and it looked like I wasn't going to see action. But the Nationals rallied for two runs in the 7th and two more in the 8th, and I was called in with two outs. I remember walking from the bullpen (located in center field) past Mantle and he said to me as I walked by, "Sully, better shut them down or we are going to miss cocktail hour." I was too nervous to reply. I threw a ground ball to the first hitter and Al Rosen booted the ball at third which tied the game. I got the side out and held the likes of Mathews, Schoendienst, Musial, Mays, Kluszewski, Logan and Aaron scoreless through the 9th, 10th and 11th.

First up in the bottom of the 12th was Stan Musial, who was at the plate laughing because Yogi (who grew up in the same area of St. Louis as Musial) is credited with saying, "For crying out loud Stan, do something. This game has gone on far too long." Musial took those words to heart, sending a high fastball into the right field stands. Later, Berra came over to my locker and said, "I should have told you he was a high fastball hitter."

The interesting thing for me was the fact that Gene Conley was the winning pitcher. He (6'8") and I (6'7") were the tallest in each league, were later traded for each other and both played basketball. There the comparisons end, as Conley played hoops at a different level. This guy went six years without a day off as he played in both the NBA and the Major Leagues. Not only that but he has championship rings in both sports and was a major contributor on every team he was on. I rank his feat right there with DiMaggio's hit streak and Ripken's endurance record.

Gene must have felt like a three-night roost in the same hotel in baseball was like a vacation compared with the travel and one-night stands of a basketball season. In those days the basketball teams traveled like gypsies and played all over the country like barnstormers while not having any chartered or private planes. I remember seeing the Celtics in the Willow Run Airport outside of Detroit at 2:00 AM waiting for a commercial plane scheduled to fly to New York at 6:30 AM because they weren't afforded rooms in town. We were just arriving on a chartered plane from Baltimore looking forward to a day off.

Needless to say, I am a big fan of the guy and think he has been short changed by the media. Someone should dial Dan Patrick or one of those other big named mouthy dudes and fill them in on this breaking news that they should have been

A typical tall and short portrayal featuring me, Whitey Ford and Nellie Fox prior to the 1955 All-Star game.

talking about for the last 40 years.

By the way, the second All-Star game I was selected to was in Washington D.C. the next year. It was a lot better. I didn't have to pitch!

Small Hotel Rooms

The Red Sox were in Baltimore and the team, as usual, was staying at the Lord Baltimore Hotel downtown. Sammy White and I had just entered our assigned room when Sam said, "I can't believe I got the key into the lock without breaking the window!" He was right, we had been assigned a very small room. In fact, Sam had been complaining about getting marginal rooms in other cities, too. "We have got to get better accommodations Sullivan! Even the @#%$^+& writers get better rooms than these closets we get. I can't sleep with my head against the wall another night and you can't be happy about your feet in that drawer."

Knowing Sam, I knew it was a challenge that he would not ignore. After breakfast the next morning and before going to the park, he said to me, "OK, grab the other end of this dresser." I said, "What?" "Just pick up the other end of this dresser, Frank, and help me carry it out into the hallway." Then, for good measure, we carried everything else out into the hall except our beds.

I could hardly wait to get back to the hotel and see what would happen. We didn't even go to dinner after the ball game before going back to check our mailbox. Sure enough there was a message that the management was sorry for any inconvenience and the furniture was back in place.

Well, that was not the message that Sam was looking for and it's too bad as I spent the next four road trips helping Sam carry all the furniture out of all the rooms we were assigned. "Jesus Christ, Sam, can't we hire Bekins Van & Storage? This is what they do and they don't have to pitch a goddamn ball game after moving furniture all morning."

Slowly the hotels got the message. First there was the polite "please don't continue to do this" and then the mild threats of telling the ball club and then the letter to the traveling secretary. To each message Sam would simply reply, "please assign us better rooms." Frank, I'll get the lamp you get the mirror." I had to admit to a personal satisfaction about the quest. It wasn't as if we weren't working for it! The gamble was, of course, would the hotels kick a whole team out with the revenue from rooms and food for 40 people three or four times a year?

The next road trip, as Sam and I boarded the bus going to the ballpark for the game against the White Sox, we overheard Mike Higgins, the rookie manager of our team, complaining about not getting the nice rooms he was getting before. We piled into the back of the bus and almost threw up trying to stifle our laughing. We had just been assigned a suite in the Del Prado Hotel on the south side of Chicago.

Not only that but there was a fruit basket and a nice note from the manager.

Barnstorming to Boston

A Major League season for a baseball player is seven months long when you throw in spring training. It's a long time to keep focused on the job at hand and there are certain players on a team who have a way of easing the grind. It is just impossible to be dead serious all the time.

Spring training for the Red Sox was in Sarasota, Florida. When it was over and it had been decided by the organization which players had, at least for the moment, made the team, they would board one of three Pullman cars attached to the back end of a train going north. Also hooked up to the train would be the cars of another team. As the train would get to a predetermined town, the five cars (we had more writers with us, thus the extra Pullman) would be put on a side track and we would play an exhibition game in that town. Then, after the game, the cars would be connected once again to the next train going north. As a young player, you would have no idea where in the hell you were. Just the fact that you were going north with the Major League team and not back to the Minor Leagues was exciting enough and who cared where the hell you were anyway.

The stops varied from nice Minor League parks to town parks with only a softball field. This meant a hastily built pitching mound with maybe a 2x4 to pitch off and the height of the mound just a wild guess. It would also mean some pretty bad infield conditions. Some of the parks were outright silly and would have been a big laugh except the infielders had to worry about being dehorned. (OK, hit in the groin.)

Each town was different and interesting. For instance at Bluefield, West Virginia, there was a scrubby looking hill behind center field where people could see over the outfield wall and not pay the price of admission. As far as I was concerned, it went both ways. You just don't get to see young barefoot girls in bib coveralls smoking corn cob pipes every day. It was Lil Abner in the flesh.

Then there was the time the umpires didn't show up. Couldn't find the town! Someone was picked out of the stands and instead of umpiring from behind the catcher because of lack of equipment, he umpired behind me on the mound. Sam White was catching and I swear to you that every pitch not hit or fouled off by the batter, he intentionally missed and let roll to the backstop. I called time. "What the hell you doing Sam? You're making me look real bad!" He glanced over his shoulder and then back at me. "See that gal behind the backstop? I'm having a real nice conversation with her and she wants to go north with us."

Sam was one of those guys that kept the team loose.

The Funniest Man I Know

In 1956, like most players when the baseball season was over, I needed to find a job to get through the winter. I had always gone home to California or played ball in Mexico or at least stayed in a warm climate, but Sam White had asked me to stay in Boston and promised we'd do pretty well on the "hot stove circuit." He also lined us up to play with the Frank Shea All-Stars, which was a team made up of Major League players from the New England area. They played about ten games in assorted towns against the local semi-pro teams before it got too cold.

As it turned out, I was surprised and delighted at how well we did. We got $100.00 a night for each game and speaking engagement and went out about every other night. Hell, it was more money than I was making playing for the Red Sox.

We were more than halfway through the winter when Sam announced we were going to Presque Isle, Maine. Believe it or not we were shuttled by Maine State Troopers from the border to Presque Isle in a blizzard. There was, from what I could see, absolutely nothing to do in that area when winter sets in. The potatoes had been planted and now it was wait until spring and be entertained in any way possible. I can assure you that White and Sullivan were any way possible. At least by now we had done a good deal of speaking and I was comfortable in front of a group of people. In fact, I was able to interject a little "Sullivan" humor and get away with it. (That means nothing was thrown.)

Upon arriving, I was shocked to see we were to be speaking in a very large auditorium to a huge audience. I said, "Sam, what the hell is going on here?" We were used to speaking to much smaller, more intimate groups and never from a stage to be the act between a tap dancer and a banjo player. Sam said, "Don't worry Sully, I'll handle everything."

I really got nervous when the tap dancer came off the stage in her "Shuffle off to Buffalo" ending. I grabbed Sam by the arm and said, "OK, what in the hell are we going to do?" He calmly looked back at me and said, "I'll take care of it, you just stay here." With that said, he strolled out on the stage and stood before the microphone and announced, "Ladies and gentlemen, my name is Sam White and I am the catcher for the Boston Red Sox. Normally I would be here to talk to you about baseball, but not tonight. Tonight, I am here to introduce the funniest man I know. In fact he is so entertaining I am coming down to sit with you. Please welcome Frank Sullivan!" and with that, he left the stage!!!!!!!!!!

P.S. Winter in Presque Isle is boring. I proved it. Nothing was thrown!

Top: Sam White, right, and I... Never trust a devil.
Bottom: A golf pro and the Frank Shea All-Stars; from left, Dick Donovan, Ron Northy, Walt Dropo, Don Hoch, me, unkown and Sam White. We really did need a lesson.

The Mouth and the Brain

I would like to tell you the entire story of Sam White and me, but since this is a children's book, I am somewhat shackled. Then again, I can tell you there was a moment at the main police station in Providence, Rhode Island, where we found ourselves trying to talk a police captain out of booking us into a jail cell. The fact that Sam was wearing a beret and had a goatee was not helping the situation.

It was the winter I stayed in Boston. We were tooling down the main drag in Providence, Rhode Island on our way to a speaking engagement at the Providence Yacht Club. There was almost no traffic and it was snowing. Sam was driving my Volkswagen Bug.

At any rate, it was not a positive thing when the captain said, "Okay, if the officer who arrested you will agree to it, I will suspend it." Red Sox fans were everywhere, but the man we were counting on was not, I fear, a Red Sox fan. Although he might have been one until... it went like this: Siren. "I want to see your identification. You're Sam White?" "Yes, officer, and I assure you I am sorry as hell about this as I know you have better things to do besides stop our little car hurrying to get to your Yacht Club to speak to those folks about Red Sox baseball." The answer was, "No, Mr. White, I have nothing better to do than arrest you for speeding!"

Sam had turned off the motor and, therefore, there was no more heat. I made the mistake to say, "Jesus, Sam, just take the *(#!%)$ ticket from the @#%$& and let's get out of here." It didn't set well with the officer, who came unglued and screamed for us to follow him back to the station. Sam liked it though, so as we followed the officer through the back streets and a lot of stop signs, Sam honked the horn and waved for him to stop. Sam motioned for the officer to open his window and then said the words that put the final nail in the coffin. "Officer, you made a lousy stop at that last sign!" I closed my eyes knowing we would be shot.

The good captain (and this sort of thing was common in that day and age) let the three of us cool down and think about our actions. Since the arresting officer would not let him suspend the charge, he doubled our fine and made us sit with the officer and apologize. Sam started by saying, "Officer, Frank's mouth works without his brain being engaged a lot and I am truly sorry about the way he acted." The officer said to Sam, as if he was now an old friend, "I think that's what's wrong with his pitching too." Then he said to me, "Why don't you just keep your mouth shut and throw hard?" I looked at the captain and he smiled and I never said another word as we walked out of there.

Bases Loaded Advice

On a hot muggy day in the middle of summer 1957, the Boston Red Sox and the biting flies from the nearby stock yards were visiting Comiskey Park on the south side of Chicago. The Red Sox were there to play the White Sox. The flies were working on somewhat more tender bodies. The weather was stifling hot and the women were using their player programs as fans. The men were wiping their torsos with the shirts they had taken off. There was the smell of Polish sausage and knockwurst and sauerkraut and marginal restrooms and sweat. It was perfect. It was baseball in the fifties and I was on the mound.

Well, not so perfect. Unfortunately, things were not going according to plan and bases were loaded. The great Nellie Fox was on third via a broken bat hit. Jim Rivera was on second with a bunt down the first base line and Jim Landis was on first by legging out an infield single. There was no one out and Minnie Minoso was at bat. For those of you who don't remember, Minnie was their best hitter. He was fearless and stood so close to the plate that you could hit him with a strike. I always felt I could get any right-handed hitter out, but Minoso could be a problem.

Sam White (my catcher) called "time out." It was OK with me! I figured he would have some situational advice and I was more than willing to listen because of the moment. What I really thought he would be reminding me about was the fact that we should pitch Minoso away because he would let an inside pitch hit him just to score a run.

The problem was that Sam chewed tobacco and spit it through his catcher's mask. I wish I could report that all of this awful slime made it cleanly through the wire when he spat but, sadly, I cannot. It was, in fact, strewn down the front of his uniform as if he had been sick to his stomach. So while I was anxious to hear his sage thoughts, I prefered he kept a reasonable distance. I motioned with both arms for him to keep at least at arms length and then cocked my ear so I could hear his ideas on how we were to proceed. He turned his head to the right and looked over at Landis on first base, then looked back at me. Then leaned his head over and looked past me to Rivera at second base, then back at me. This was taking some time and I'm was getting a little edgy waiting for him to say something, but he merely looked now at Fox on third base and again back at me. Finally he took his dripping mask off, looked back at home plate where Minoso waited, then again back at me and said his only words before leaving the mound, "Jesus Christ! You're in a lot of trouble!"

All of which, I believe, proves that bad news doesn't always travel fast.

The Gal at the Brewery

Friday, March 22, 1957, was more than another day on the calendar for me and, in fact, the Bay Area of San Francisco was really shook up about it too.

It was my fourth year with the Red Sox and we had traveled from our training camp in Sarasota, Florida, to rainy New Orleans; played the Cleveland Indians in an exhibition game in the mud and continued by air to San Francisco. There the team checked into a hotel about two blocks from Union Square on Geary Street.

A fraternity friend of mine picked me up and we went out to the Lucky Lager Brewery where he worked as director of sales and marketing. I was attentive and alert. After all it was a brewery! Then while passing through the offices, I spotted a very good looking tall girl. You know, elbow in the ribs, hey buddy, why don't you ask her if she'd like to meet me after the game at the Iron Horse (famous San Francisco watering hole). We then had a sampling of the Lucky Lager product because I wasn't pitching and he drove me back to the hotel.

I found my roommate, Sam White, talking with Joe Cronin, the general manager of the Red Sox and Hall of Fame shortstop, in the lobby. I said hello to Joe and then Sam and I got on the elevator and were about to punch in the 6th floor, when we saw a very elderly lady supported by two canes obviously struggling to make the same elevator.

One of the greatest things about being with Sam in those days was the fact that he always went out of his way for the elderly and this moment was no exception. I held the door open and Sam moved out to meet her. After getting her aboard, it turned out she was going to the same 6th floor. When the door opened, we got on either side and half-carried her from the elevator and all the way down the hall past our room to hers at the end of the hallway. She was very impressed with our service and told us so.

We were only in our room minutes and I had just read a message that said the gal at the brewery would meet me after the game when the Richter scale registered 5.3 and the building was doing the hula!

Sam, unlike me, had never been in an earthquake and was unnerved. Naturally, I was unaffected. Although I imagine it might have looked the contrary as I raced wide-eyed for the doorway shouting, "For God's sake Sam follow me!" I had been trained by my parents to stand in the door jamb in an earthquake.

As we stood in the open doorway, we were delighted to see the same old lady go sprinting by us without a cane in sight heading for the exit stairs.

Oh, by the way, I married the gal I met at the Iron Horse.

Shaking off the Signal

The baseball term for a pitch thrown as hard as a fastball, but released with a clockwise twist of the wrist without much spin, is called a "slider." It breaks late, slightly down and away from a right-hand batter if thrown by a right-hand pitcher.

Because I was very comfortable with the pitch, I took it another step by changing speeds and also throwing it for my "control pitch" (Got to have a strike) and stayed 10 years in the Major Leagues. When pitchers got into trouble back then, most would rely on a fastball for a strike. Their odds weren't as good.

Roy Sievers was a power hitter for the Washington Senators and in 1958 he hit 39 home runs and, in his 16-year Major League career, he hit 318. Roy was one of the many great hitters who went to the batter's box with a definite plan.

For instance in 1956, the first time Roy came to the plate in a game being played in the old Griffith Stadium in Washington, D.C., I started off by throwing a slow slider for a strike and he took the pitch without swinging. I threw another slider with the same result. With two strikes on him I threw a fastball low and away for a ball and then came back on the next pitch with a slider, which he took for strike three. He sat down and I felt good all over.

His next time at the plate, I started him off with a hard slider for a strike, which again he took without swinging. I then threw an easy slider that missed the outside of the plate for a ball. Next pitch, I threw him another hard slider for a strike that he took again. Unbelievably, he took the next really hard slider for strike three. He sat down and I felt so good that little babies could play with me.

His final time in the batter's box is the reason you have had to suffer the last two paragraphs. He took strike one as my slider cut the outside corner. He took strike two looking at the same pitch. I wasted a fastball low and away and, when Sammy White, my catcher, called for another slider I thought, "Surely, he will know I am coming back with another slider," so I shook off Sam who wanted me to throw another slider and threw Sievers a fastball strike and he quickly hit it fifteen rows up in the bleachers. It was the pitch he had been waiting for all game long and the only one he swung at. His reward was 1 RBI, a batting average of .333 for the day and proof that his method worked. My reward was having to listen to Sammy say, "If you are going to start thinking this late in your career Sullivan, simply stop the game and let's talk!" My reply won't be printed at this time but it had to do with him trying an extraordinary sex act with himself.

Vic Wertz

Every batter in baseball, at one time or another, must face a pitcher he wishes would drop dead on the spot. Check that! He would prefer to hammer him into the ground with his bat! Conversely, every pitcher must throw to a batter he wishes had an instant bowel problem. Check that! Make it menstrual cramps.

Vic Wertz, when he played first base for Cleveland, hit everything I threw as if he knew beforehand what pitch was coming and what speed I had dialed in. It got to be so bad that I asked my first and second basemen to bring notes from their wives to say they understood the situation; after all, their husbands were risking their manhood! To make matters worse, Vic was a nice guy. (Became a teammate in 1958 with the Red Sox.)

If you watch the World Series on TV, it's a good bet you will have to suffer again through the Willie Mays over-the-shoulder catch again in the 1954 Series played at the Polo Grounds in New York. It was Vic who hit that long ball. I always watch it with a smile because it is the only time I get to see one of his shots being caught. Vic played 16 years in the Major Leagues and was a .277-lifetime hitter, but if he could have had more at bats off me, he would have had a batting average rivaling Ty Cobb and been a first ballot Hall of Famer. In fact, if the American League had been full of batters like Vic, I would have had to go to work for a living.

The year after Cleveland went to the World Series, Vic had a bout with polio that put his career in jeopardy. I sent him a telegram saying that I would forego worrying him about cutting me in on his World Series check (since I was partly responsible for their great season) if he would just answer my prayers and get well. Later, when I found out Vic was beating the polio, I sent him another telegram saying, "On the other hand, if you're going to live and still be able to hit, forget the first message."

Vic beat the polio and returned to Cleveland the next year. When they came to Boston the first time, Vic found me during batting practice and thanked me for caring. I told him, jokingly, the only reason I did it was so I could ask him what he saw in my throwing that allowed him to pound me like he did. I was shocked when he willingly said it seemed that I had stopped throwing fastballs at him in the clutch and he could just lay off that pitch and wait for the slower breaking stuff.

From then on, when I pitched against Vic, I never threw him another fastball in a tight situation and he never hit a ball out of the park off me again.

It really is a fascinating game.

Top: Vic Wertz, Gene Stephens and Gary Geiger.
Bottom: Ted Williams, left, and Ty Cobb at spring training.

Bored

For seven months professional baseball players need to eat good, drink within reason, get plenty of rest and show up on time to compete every day. Managing the time between games is a huge priority for successful players. I know because boredom almost got me killed one afternoon while sitting on the steps of the Red Sox dugout concentrating on killing ants one by one with my forefinger when Williams hit a screaming foul ball into our dugout that missed my head by inches.

Unfortunately, as a starting pitcher and slated to be on the mound every fourth day, I was hard pressed to wile away countless hours with nothing to do but be ready when called on. I loved being at the park every day to work out to keep in shape but when I played, we were not allowed to engage in any other sport including swimming, golf or fishing except on rare off days. If I had it to do over again I would make a schedule for each day and spend the winter months developing that agenda because I was constantly seeking alternative things to keep from going mad! How many times can you go to an Abercrombie & Fitch store only to find out you can't afford (in the '50s) the unbelievably good stuff offered and most of the goodies were summer related anyway, meaning I would never get the chance to use the thing because of my profession.

Then, I realized the browsing put a huge stress on the legs, just as in the minor leagues when you went to the pool hall for countless games of losing to the best pool player on the team who would never make it to the Major Leagues because he spent too much time on his feet around the pool table.

I remember a time in Scranton when there was a BB gun fight inside a boarding house because it was fun. While playing for Boston, Vic Wertz and I had a bag full of slot cars for road trips. I found a horse race game on a vibrating table that caused half the Red Sox team to be cited by the Scottsdale Police for "fan" noise at a late hour. In the Minor Leagues I was shocked when I was told by a teammate that the rope ladder would be in place to escape the mezzanine of the hotel in Fresno, California. In the late '40s it was common for the hotels to house a Minor League team on the second floor that afforded a view of the lobby below where the team manager would be to curtail any out of hotel activities. Cots would be set up for the whole team except for the manager and the bus driver/trainer who had rooms. Luckily, I didn't use the ladder that night because the drain pipe the ladder was hung from broke and the only thing that saved our second baseman was some trash cans below. Luckily it caused little hurt except in his wallet, as the manager heard the racket and intercepted him coming out of the back alley.

The Night Before the Game

Don Larsen was a friend of mine before he pitched the perfect game in the 1956 World Series. When I first arrived in the Majors in 1953, I watched him pitch and hit a home run in Fenway Park when he was with the St. Louis Browns. You remember the St. Louis Browns. They used to be the farthest team west in the American League until becoming the Baltimore Orioles in 1954.

I met Don after the 1953 Major League season in Mexico. We both played for Ciudad Obregon and he played left field when he wasn't pitching and hit 20 home runs. Don was fun to be with, especially if you were thirsty.

In 1955, Whitey Ford, Bob Lemon and I were tied with league high 18 wins. They had pitched their last games but I was slated to pitch the first game of a season-ending meaningless double header with the Yankees, who had already clinched the title and were World Series bound. We were solidly mired in fourth place. As my wife points out now, I could have won the most games that year, but while baseball seems to be a game of statistics, I can assure you that very few players in my time gave a living hoot about them. In fact, as most of us reflect on the past and realize that numbers seem to be how a player is judged now, we are aghast. We played to win and little else!

So when Don called me when the Yankees came into town and said let's dine, I said sure, willingly disregarding a self rule that no alcohol was to be consumed 24 hours prior to pitching. Do I need to go on? Need I tell you that it is very difficult to sneak around Boston if you are 6' 7" and your pal is 6' 4" and both of you play in the Major Leagues. Must I explain that most New Englanders, living above Providence, Rhode Island, live and die with the Red Sox, especially against the hated Yankees? I was playing with dynamite and felt it and, in fact, broke it off early so as not to be seen "out about town" late.

Next day I felt the effects of the evening. There was no adrenalin pumping. I couldn't get fired up. First pitch I threw, Coleman hit it off the wall. Honestly, I was thrilled because I got it over the plate! Second pitch, McDougald did the same. Okay, we had a problem here. Then Hank Bauer ripped one into the gap between left and center. Throwing strikes is normally a positive. This time it was killing me. In fact, Mickey Mantle, who wasn't playing, got to the top step of their dugout and hollered at me, "What are you trying to do Sully? Beat the traffic?"

Well, I didn't win number 19, but I did find out that if I wasn't sharp, rested and fired up, it would translate into not pitching well. On the other hand, if I wanted to beat the traffic, Mantle understood the formula.

The Danger of Pitching

Herb Score, while pitching for Cleveland, was hit in the eye by Gil McDougald of the Yankees with a line drive and was lucky to live. Being only 60' 6" from home plate it is more than a little dangerous, but I never knew a pitcher who spent even one moment worrying about it.

When Bob Cerv played for the Kansas City Royals, he became a very scary straight away hitter. In his case, we all knew it and were ready. It was the unexpected line drive that was the problem.

My problem was pitching against Al Kaline, the Detroit Tigers great. He had trouble pulling the ball to left field off me. The result was his solid hits came straight back through the middle. While this did keep the ball in the park, it also reduced my safety factor greatly. In fact, three of his "at bats" against me were very painful experiences. In a tight game in Detroit, I threw Al a slider as hard as I could which forced me to lose sight of him for a split second. He lined the ball directly at my head. As I turned my head quickly back at him, I caught sight of the ball in time to throw my glove hand and my bare hand in front of my right temple catching it, but the force of the blow knocked me down. While the catch ended the inning and had Al fuming, it also had me wondering if I would be able to continue because the ball had struck my right forefinger. Luckily, we had a big inning and I got the feeling back in the finger enough to pitch the last inning and win.

The very next time I pitched against him was terribly embarrassing. After throwing him a very hard low fastball on the outside of the plate, my follow-through half turned me around and he hit a ball that hit me in the butt. After picking the ball up and throwing him out, I staggered awkwardly around the pitching mound trying not to rub it in front of the fans. Harvey Kuenn, their shortstop, hollered from the bench, "I know you're confused after being hit in the brain like that."

In another game, he hit a line drive off my left shin bone that went all the way into our dugout on the fly. I could not finish the game. I just knew it was broken, but x-rays were negative. I was on crutches for three days and I had to slit my pant leg to get my trousers on. Kaline, the cheap bastard, ignored my bill for the slacks.

Then there was the time my teammate, Joe Tully, pitching for the San Jose Red Sox in 1948 against the Yankee farm team in Ventura, California, absorbed a line drive to the crotch that bent his metal cup inside out. Needless to say, he fell face down on the mound and when he woke up our catcher said, "Don't worry Joe, San Jose has a girl's team you can pitch for."

Chess with Curt Gowdy

The game of chess is a game every child should be made aware of. It is a game that requires the knowledge that each piece moves according to different rules and therefore requires a different approach to winning; proving, I hope, that there is "more than one way to skin a cat." (I'm trying to remember the last cat skinning.) I used to play the game of chess with Curt Gowdy while on road trips in the early 1950s. Curt spent most of his off hours lying on a piece of plywood in his hotel room hoping the firmness would cure his already ruined spine in the days he was the radio (play-by-play) sportscaster for the Boston Red Sox. Curt was a good guy, despite not being afraid to further his career. Personally, I would rate him in the top three of the all time great sports broadcasters.

The chess games were played without a time limit for moves because we had plenty of time but, I assure you, we didn't need a whole lot of time as both of us played a very aggressive style.

I remember a game we had in his room in the Del Prado Hotel on the south side of Chicago. The hotel staff had brought him exactly what he had requested which was a 4' X 8' piece of 1/4" plywood and placed it on his bed. I sat on the other bed and, in our haste to play the game, Curt didn't put a blanket or anything on the wood and how his right elbow got through the next 2 hours I will never know. It really demonstrates the type of guy he was.

Once, while I was recovering from pneumonia, I was asked by Curt to sit for a few innings in the Fenway Park radio booth and comment on the game. I must tell you it was a new look at what I was playing. It was as if the game had nothing to do with the complex personalities who gathered together for each game and tried to compete against each other. It was THE GAME! It was a shock to me that it was so visually clear that some players made the easy catch and some couldn't and it was very clear who wasn't doing the job.

I found sportscasters in those days were dedicated, interesting and competent. None of them were burdened with an analyst and very few criticized. Every word out of their mouth was digested by the most avid of the fans and when they wove their oral magic we delighted in the comfort of it all. What could be better than working on a little project in the garage and listening to a Jack Buck? What could be better than the voice of Vin Scully painting the picture of the game in our minds while driving the freeways of this country? What could be better than sailing New England waters with the radio tuned to a game done by Curt Gowdy? For those of you who didn't get the chance to do that, "Nothing" is the answer.

A Remarkable Photo Shoot

In the summer of 1956, while playing for the Red Sox, we got a rare day off but I was told to take my uniform and go to Stockbridge, Massachusetts, to be photographed along with Sam White and Jackie Jensen. We were given no choice and were told to furnish our own transportation. When we looked and found out it was a three-hour drive just to get there and the gas money was on us, you had three guys semi-hot. Who the hell did this guy think he was?

Jensen volunteered to drive and came by my place with White already in the car. So, off we went to the southwest corner of the state. Stockbridge is about halfway between Springfield, Massachusetts, and Albany, New York, on your map, some 140 miles out of Boston.

On arrival, we found the address and were greeted warmly by a small slim man smoking a pipe and his name meant nothing to me. We lunched with him and a few friends of his at a nice restaurant off the main drag and then went over to a two story wooden building with a studio on the second floor. There we put our uniforms on and Jensen and I were told to sit side by side on a bench with my arm on Jensen's shoulder while Jackie faked tying his shoe lace. It was explained to us that the Sarasota, Florida, locker room we used in spring training would be the background. Sam was photographed separately. Then the man said Ted Williams refused to make the drive but would permit him to paint his face in. So, I was also asked to stand in a different pose leaning on a wall where Williams would have stood. It all took a while and was a little confusing.

Well, anyway, it was semi-interesting and we got through it and headed back to "Beantown." I remember sitting in the back seat ragging on Jensen about all this being his fault. "Really great, Jack! Drive us halfway across the nation to meet a photographer who doesn't seem sure what the hell he is doing." Sam chimed in, "Sad affair, Jack. Finally get a day off and not a soul mentions anything to drink before lunch stronger than ice tea."

Moral of the story is there are times a guy should just shut up and do what is asked because the following year, there we were, right in the middle of the cover for the Saturday Evening Post magazine issue dated March 2, 1957 and there was my body with a bad looking Williams head on it. The man was an illustrator not a portrait artist and, if you'll look closely, you'll see we are wearing street shoes, not spikes.

The cover was titled "The Rookie." The man's name turned out to be Norman Rockwell.

A Police Escort

It was a depressing day when I heard they tore down Briggs Stadium in Detroit. When I played there with the Red Sox, the visiting locker room was bad. The shower room was pitiful and the dugout was awful because most players couldn't stand up straight and it only had seats for about 12 guys comfortably.

Hitters drooled when they saw the place. Both left and right fields were short and there was hardly any foul ball territory for anyone to catch a foul ball in, plus the hitting background was great. Good pitchers drooled because the center field fence was about $4.00 in a cab. The biggest plus I felt was the backstop was right behind the catcher and the visual effect was like being right on top of the hitter.

The hotel we stayed in was about 5 city blocks from Briggs. I used to walk there with other players rather than take the team bus or a cab. The walk went through the "slum part of town" and when it was my turn to pitch, it was common for me to hear from men slumped against the concrete wall of a building, with their bottle in a sack saying, "Good luck Sullivan;" "Stay strong son;" "Make yourself proud boy." They must have always read the paper they sat on. There were times I wanted to say, "Save me a place if I don't get this done."

Another unique thing about the place was the number of police cars in the private parking lot that the players and management used inside the property fence. The concession kitchens seemed to be operating all the time and I would see Detroit's "finest" eating in one of the lighted rooms as I walked by under the stands in right field to get to the locker room. The reason I bring this up is to try and explain why I was not thrown in jail in that fine town.

I had pitched a shutout against Jim Bunning and we had won 1 to 0 as Ted Williams hit a home run. I was constantly in trouble in that game. Every inning was like Custer's last stand with a different ending. Our right fielder, Jackie Jensen, threw out two guys at home plate while Bunning was his usual self, mowing down our hitters, until Ted Williams did his usual act in Briggs Stadium.

To say the least I was elated. Stayed too long around a case of National Bohemian beer and somehow had been given a car to get back to the hotel.

The policeman said, "Sullivan! You are going the wrong way on a one-way street. I'm commandeering this vehicle and you are coming with me." He had his partner take the car back to the park and he took me into the hotel, up the elevator and when I finally got the door opened he said, "Keep beating my team and this sort of thing will stop! Goodnight kid."

I fear that this sort of behavior might be handled differently now. How sad!

Insulting Tom Yawkey

George Page wanted his 42-foot Convertible Flying Bridge Chris-Craft power boat taken to Fort Lauderdale, Florida, and he wanted it there as fast as possible. I couldn't wait and, when the baseball season was over, I was ready for the 1600 mile trip. This boat had twin gas engines which made it fast but troublesome. Back then (1958) when gas engines were in high RPM all day, they were less than reliable when throttled back and would, in fact, quit while maneuvering to a dock if brought back to idle. So, a person needed to anticipate this ugly event.

The reason I bring this up is because Sam White wanted to go along. Sam was a fabulous athlete, but when it came to steering a boat or using clutches and throttles I would have been better off with an ape! I left him at the wheel one day in South Carolina while I desperately made it down to the head. Upon returning to the bridge, I found us not moving forward because it is impossible to travel in 36 inches of water if a boat draws 4 feet. I asked Sam what the *#%$%^ was he thinking? He said, "You never said think, you said steer!" I looked and he had the inland waterway chart upside down!

Thankfully, it was all sandy silt and when the tide came in we managed to free up easily. Watching the temperature gauges closely (mud clogging the water intakes might overheat the engines), we retraced our path back to the waterway and deeper water and all was well again.

I was told when we left New England that Tom Yawkey, owner of the Red Sox, owned an island off the South Carolina coast. Just south of Georgetown are a number of islands and, sure enough, one of them is called Cat Island and, yes, Tom Yawkey was the owner. Nothing to do but stop and see our boss, right? After a quick stop we called and damn if we weren't invited. I pulled the boat up to a very long pier and out came 2 WWII jeeps. Mrs. Yawkey was with them and warmly greeted us. We were taken to the main complex for drinks and dinner, but not before Mr. Yawkey himself showed us his island game reserve.

After a great dinner with much wine and many laughs, we retired into the trophy room and settled around some superior brandy. One drink led to another and the conversation somehow settled around hitting and, the next thing I knew, Mr. Yawkey had a broom in his hands and was showing Sam what he thought was wrong with Sam's swing. Honestly, fearing the worst, I did everything in my power to get them off the subject, but to no avail. I heard Sam tell our host, "You may be right Tom, but if I was that fat I'd never get around to the ball."

I have never been in a room where people sobered more quickly.

At the Key Club with Sam

In 1960 Bucky Harris had become the general manager of the Boston Red Sox. Bucky drank like a camel going on safari, and I can't remember ever getting to talk to him. It figured. I had a hard time getting over the pneumonia of the year before and the lousy year that went with it. In professional sports, when a player isn't doing well, everyone will shy away except close friends and hecklers.

Spring training was in Scottsdale, Arizona which was like a prison for me. Like Bucky, the desert and I had nothing to talk about. Sam White was there but his mind really wasn't into it as he had just opened his 48 lane bowling alley in Brighton, Massachusetts, and was considering retirement. Sam found out that Bucky had loaned a Boston sportswriter a key club card. It didn't take long for Sam to con the writer out of it for the afternoon. After our morning workout at the ballpark, Sam asked me if I'd like a beer. That's like asking that same camel if he wanted the water, and Sam pulled this key card out of his pocket and said follow me.

After settling down at a very nice table in the middle of the room, Sam, for the very first time I could remember, seemed totally relaxed (he normally was always on the prowl) and, as the afternoon wore on, I could sense he was content with his decision to hang up the spikes. For me, it wasn't like just another guy at the end of his playing career. We had been like brothers for seven years. We competed together as 'well' as a pitcher/catcher tandem ever did. After the third inning Sam would catch me without signals because we were so in-tune. We never had a serious moment off the field. Hell, I loved the guy!

For those of you who don't know or forgot, the tab at a key club always went to the owner of the key and there was no cash exchange for anything. Well, it was brutal. One $3.00 beer led to another until the band showed up and the price went up. It was then that Sam started including the band with every round of beers.

A few hours later I can dimly remember the top of the upright piano being stacked solid with beer mugs and the trumpet player trying to play with the mouthpiece in his nose. When I woke up the next morning I had to look into my wallet to find out who I was. Simply stated, I had a massive overhang! Not to worry, just go to the park and start running. It impresses the management and it's amazing (when you're young) how you can sweat it out.

No matter, there was big trouble! Seems the bill we had rung up was in excess of Bucky's budget and Sam was traded to the Cleveland Indians for Russ Nixon, and I'm sure my being with Sam hadn't warmed Bucky's heart either. To make matters worse, Bucky hired Billy Jurges as manager. Billy couldn't manage a smile much less a team.

Short Stories

Frank Malzone, playing third base for the Red Sox in Washington's Griffith Stadium, came to the mound while I was pitching and said, "I've had enough ground balls, let someone else get a few." Neither of us realized he had just tied the league record for assists in one game.

Once again in that Washington ballpark on an extremely hot and humid afternoon, we were playing in front of no more than 2,000 people (maybe less) when a fight broke out between the only two men sitting in the left field bleachers. We stopped the game and watched the two go at it for 5 minutes.

Ted Williams and Gus Zernial (playing for the Athletics) put on a ten swing home run hitting contest in Philadelphia. Gus hit all 5 swings over the wall with 3 going over the roof in left field. Williams hit his first 4 swings over the wall in right field, but Gus was declared the winner when Ted's last effort hit the clock over the scoreboard in right field about $4.00 in a cab ride away.

One day in the Old Park in Atlanta, Ga. (below the train yards) it was so cold that those of us pitching as relievers for the Birmingham Barons (AA ball at the time) were issued coffee cans with a couple of glowing charcoal cubes in them to be put under a blanket for warmth. In the game Joe DeMaestri went to his left at shortstop to field a ground ball that took a bad hop. It caught him on his metal protector and the noise resounded and echoed in that frozen place like a bell had been rung. From then on, throughout the Red Sox organization, it was known as "The bell in the dell."

I threw a pitch to Mickey Mantle in a game in Yankee Stadium who popped it up so high that when Frank Malzone finally caught the thing Mickey kicked third base. Malzone complained of a sore neck from looking straight up so long.

Ellis Kinder didn't get to the Major Leagues until he was over 30 years old and by then he was a dedicated Scotch drinker. The Scots are still living off his purchases. Getting the man ready to pitch on days he was in the bullpen wasn't an easy task, especially when he would have to be awakened to warm up. No matter. Once awakened he was outstanding with incredible control of every pitch imaginable in those days. Like so many others, one can only wonder what he could have been baseball-wise if there hadn't been a WWII.

I shouted (a mere professional critique) at an umpire in Detroit on a day I wasn't pitching and when I realized he was coming over to our visitor's dugout to throw me out of the game, I bolted out the right side and ran as fast as I could to our bullpen in right field. He stopped and had a laugh and I saved $75.00.

Top: *After another victory, Billy Klaus, Billy Goodman, Ellis Kinder and I.*
Bottom: *Myself, Gil McDougald and Frank Malzone at a Boston Sports Writers award dinner.*

Practice with the Boston Celtics

In the winter of 1956 Jack Nichols was the center for the Boston Celtics when Bill Russell was acquired for that team. Russell could stand flat-footed and jump straight up and touch the rim with both elbows. Jack was no fool and opted for finishing dental school and promised Red Auerbach he would be available for the games, but not practice. He told Red his neighbor would take his place in practice.

It was the winter that Sam White asked me to stay in the east and do speaking engagements with him. After the baseball season was over, Jackie Jensen left for California and I moved into his house only a few houses away from Sam's. Sam had been an All-American basketball player for the University of Washington and a teammate of Jack Nichols. At a party at Sam's house, I was introduced to Nichols and it turned out he was my neighbor. He said he knew Sam was tied up, but Sam had told him I could play a little. Would I mind helping him out?

This was the Celtics' first championship year. They were 44 - 28 and the roster read like this: Bob Cousy - Tom Heinsohn - Dick Hemric - Jim Loscutoff - Jack Nichols - Togo Palazzi - Andy Phillip - Frank Ramsey - Arnie Risen - Bill Russell - Bill Sharman - Lou Tsioropoulos.

Talk about a group. Cousy, Heinsohn, Ramsey, Russell and Sharman have had their numbers retired by the team. All of them, plus Risen, are in the Basketball Hall of Fame. Cousy was the league's Most Valuable Player that year and Heinsohn was the league's Rookie of the Year.

Well, besides being a zero fat tolerance game, one seems to need an extra lung to compete at the professional level in that sport. I found myself somewhat removed from the physical shape needed to compete with the above roster when I agreed to take Nichols' place in the Celtics practice. Our speaking engagements were not without adult beverages and bedtime proved to be considerably past the glass slipper number but, once again, my mouth overloaded my ass!

Two things kept happening. 1. Every time I was chosen to be on one team in practice, the other team clapped. 2. I always wound up guarding Heinsohn and it sounded like this: "Oops sorry Sully. Let me help you up. You're not bleeding are you pal? Jesus, I didn't mean to step on your foot buddy. Damn, Sully I had no idea my elbow could make a welt like that. Godammit Frank, I didn't mean to put you that far into the seats. Come on, get up and I'll buy you a beer after practice."

Auerbach played me all pre-season and asked me to think about playing two sports. I thanked him, but told him I thought my butt was already "maxed" out.

Getting Paid for Fishing

It was 1957 and the last game of the season had been played in Washington, D.C. The Red Sox three Pullman cars were attached to a train going north to Boston. I was walking to my roomette when I passed Ted Williams' compartment. The door was open and he spotted me and hollered, "Hey Sully, come on in!"

I sat down and he said, "You had another pretty good year and I was talking to Joe Cronin (general manager) the other day and he told me to tell you to stop by his office when you get back. I think he is going to give you a check that can help you get through the winter."

In my mind I hadn't had that good a season with a record of 14 and 11. So I was surprised to hear I was going to get a bonus (which turned out to be $2,000), although I was second on the team in wins behind Tom Brewer who led the staff with 16 wins, and my earned run average had been a respectable 2.73.

Williams was relaxed and in a good mood. Hell, he ought to have been; he had won the American League batting title hitting .388 at age 38 to become the oldest to ever do it. It was also the year the team moved up in the standings and finished third in the league behind the Yankees and White Sox.

I asked Ted what he was going to do for the coming winter and he said he was going home to Islamorada in the Florida Keys and was also looking forward to fishing for salmon up in New Brunswick, but first he had to fly to Seattle and spend a week at a Sportsman Show where he and Jack Sharkey would be putting on demonstrations of fly casting. He asked me what I was going to do and I told him about the 38' ketch-rigged sailboat I had bought and was going to sail to Florida. He thought I was nuts and said so, but also said that if I got lucky and made it all the way down his way to stop in and he'd take me fishing. He then launched into the subject of fishing.

Next to hitting a baseball, at which he was the best I ever saw, Ted considered himself to have no peers when it came to fishing. In his eyes, fishing was not a leisurely pastime. It was to be attacked without the aid of a single beer from dawn to fading light. His idea of lunch while fishing was an apple washed down with water! Are you kidding me? Once started on the subject he would go on forever.

I finally found a moment to break away and told him I was going to hit the sack and, as I walked out of his compartment I said, "By the way Ted, what do they pay you for the fishing thing in Seattle?" He said, "$15,000, why?" "Oh, I was just wondering, see you in the morning."

As I walked down the narrow passage to my roomette it was hard to swallow the fact that $15,000 was what I had just been paid to play the whole season.

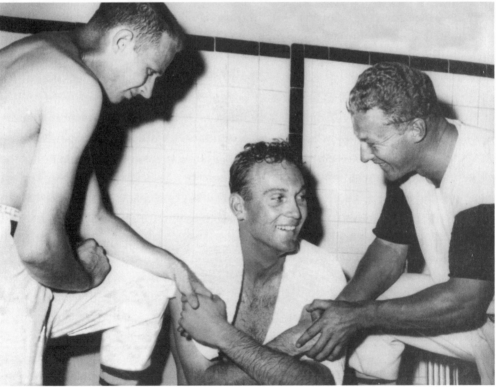

*Top: I asked Vic Wertz, Frank Malzone and Pete Runnels if I could join them in the picture.
They said they wouldn't mind as long as I didn't have a bat in my hand. Teammates can be
cruel at times.*
*Bottom: While Jackie Jensen's hand shake was sincere, my pal Gene Stephens' grip seemed to
say I was lucky to win the game. Teammates can be cruel at times.*

Pete Runnels and the Hypnotist

Jackie Jensen was a great ball player, but there seemed to be very little about the life that a ball player lived that appealed to him. In the mid-fifties, as baseball teams started moving into the west, teams had to fly to make schedules. Jackie hated flying and between a marriage going bad and flying, the thrill (if there ever was one for him) was gone completely and he retired.

Pete Runnels and I were distraught. What the hell were we going to do about great dinners in fancy restaurants with Jensen gone. Jensen, who owned the Bow & Bell Restaurant in Jack London Square in Oakland, was normally afforded complimentary or reciprocal dining opportunities in the finest eateries across the land. At worst, he would flash his credit card and pass it off as deductible. Pete and I were his constant companions in cities like New York, where we would chat with the likes of Robert Preston, Sammy Davis Jr. and Sterling Haden in Danny's Hideaway, which featured no menu. Just order and they would get it.

The Red Sox 1960 spring training was in Scottsdale, Arizona and our first exhibition game after breaking camp was to be in Las Vegas. Pete and I couldn't stand it so we wired Jackie. "Meet us in Las Vegas and bring your credit card." Then we sent a second one that read, "If you can't make it, send the card!"

Damn if he didn't show up. After the game, we took Don Buddin (shortstop) along and went onto the strip and had dinner in a fine restaurant with Dr. Arthur Allen (hypnotist) who had tried to help Jackie with the flying problem. Pete, after a couple of drinks, started to question the doctor because as far as Pete was concerned hypnosis was bull#$@%. Finally, Pete let the doctor know what he thought and, I assure you, it wasn't complimentary. So, nothing to do but go to his show and see what would happen. True to his word, Dr. Allen put us on the stage and before Pete could finish telling me this guy was full of %$#@ he was out cold. I turned to my right to tell Buddin but it was no use. Everyone but me was out of it. Dr. Allen then put his hand on my forehead but it was no use. It wasn't that I didn't want to. It just didn't work. Probably too dense.

At any rate, he had them do silly things and then started waking them up one at a time. When he got to Pete and, before he woke him up, he placed his hand on Pete's head and told him he would have the best baseball season of his career and for him to just relax and enjoy it. We barely got out of the place before Pete started talking about the guy being full of #$@% again. In fact he never would concede that the man was legitimate, even after I told him what he had been doing on the stage, but he won the American League batting title that season.

Scrap Iron Gets Married

Clinton Dawson Courtney, nicknamed "Scrap Iron." Born 03/16/27 in Hall Summit, Louisiana. Top ten on the list of my all-time characters.

Played for the Yankees in '51, Cardinals '52-53, Orioles '54, White Sox '55, Senators '55-59, Orioles '60, Athletics '61, and back to the Orioles same year.

Clint was 5'8" tall, about 180 lbs. A catcher by trade but would play anywhere needed and would break one of your bones to win. One of the only catchers in those days who wore glasses while catching. He only had one pair as long as I knew him. They were simple, round, metal framed glasses. They could only be described as ugly, ill-fitting, bent, scratched and never cleaned. To tell you that he didn't give a damn what you thought is a waste of time. Scrap Iron was the type of player who would let you hit him in the Adam's apple when he was batting, just to get on base. When I faced him in games, he would not acknowledge that he knew me when the game was in progress. It was only later after a cooling down period that he would nod and say hello.

I first met him in Mazatlan, Mexico where I joined the Ciudad Obregon team on the road. Clint was the manager because he could speak Spanish fluently. In fact I roomed with him that night. Hard to forget as he simply stood by his bed, dropped his entire ensemble on the floor with his cowboy boots standing up through the trouser leg holes. In the morning he stood in the boots and simply pulled the entire ensemble up in place.

One day in the city of Culiacan, Clint pulled us off the field because the umpires were so bad and a sheriff put a cocked gun to his chest and said, "Señor Courtney, you will play the game!" Scraps said in Spanish, "Up your bucket! AMIGO!"

Clint got married that year in Obregon to his Louisiana sweetheart. She was an absolute fireball and between the two of them it was not really a marriage but more of a collision. After the wedding, conducted in the side door of the local Catholic Church since they were not Catholic, Clint and his bride were sitting side by side at the head table at the reception when a telegram arrived from a señorita who seemed to think she had first dibs on Scrap Iron. We all flinched as Clint read the telegram out loud to the crowd and then kissed the paper it was written on. Well, he didn't even get the telegram out of the way before being cartwheeled right over the back of his chair. She hit him with a closed fist right between the right lens and the left lens. After pawing around on the floor until he found his glasses and bleeding slightly from the nose, he stood up, put his arm around his bride and said, "Damn darling, I thought you could hit harder than that!"

Record Runs from East to West

In Texas, I drove the 293 miles from Van Horn to Del Rio without seeing another moving vehicle! Granted, I had started in El Paso at 2:00 AM, but still!

I was on my way to spring training in Florida from Burbank, California, in 1953 and that day I drove all the way from El Paso to Lafayette, Louisiana, before stopping to see a cousin. That's right, all the way across Texas in one day alone. Tired? If my cousin had served soup, I would have drowned.

In the early fifties, there was nothing like starting out on a trip across our nation alone. You had to be sure your vehicle was road worthy because there were great distances between help, but it was exciting to intentionally break from your present situation and go to another phase of your life. It was also a time when I found there where stretches of this country I really didn't care if I ever saw again.

Twenty-three years old, alone, with a good car and nothing but open road and freedom to deal with, it was exciting. I found that by using the neck strap off my camera case wound around the steering yoke to support my right knee, made it easier to keep the pedal-to-the-metal before "cruise control" was invented for states like Indiana that didn't have a speed limit then.

With my proud father with me in 1957, I bought a top of the line Oldsmobile 98 right off the showroom floor in Burbank, my home town. It had a visor over the windshield and an automatic headlight dimmer and it was advertised that you could run it full throttle all day long. Without my proud father with me, I paid my toll on a 100-mile road between Tulsa and Oklahoma City while going from east to west one fall day and the man who collected the dollar said to me, "Son, you better slow down a bit because you just did that in one hour."

I remember a drive across the country when I was tooling down the New Jersey Turnpike before turning west on the Pennsylvania Turnpike following a little dark green (back wheels looked bow-legged) Volkswagen Bug with a U.S. Forestry logo on the door. There were two young guys in it and they had the thing going wide open (68 mph). With my big car I thought I'd lose them. Wrong! I'd see them go by every time I stopped for gas. I finally got rid of them around Albuquerque. Unfortunately, I had the funny feeling that it was their destination.

My record run alone between Boston, Massachusetts, and Burbank was 3 1/2 days. A few years later my Red Sox rookie teammate, Jim Pagliaroni, dropped me off at Boston's Logan airport in his cut down "Olds 88" and showed up at my house in Burbank in three days flat.

Now why would he have wanted to do that? Damn kids!

Tom Brewer

After spending the winter in Boston in 1956, it was time to drive south to Sarasota, Florida, to spring training with the Red Sox. Austin Thomas Brewer lived somewhat along the way and had always said, "Come on by." I called and asked if they would mind a visit. His wife, Barbara, said it was mandatory. Tom, pitching for the Boston Red Sox from 1954 to 1961 was fearless. He won 91 games and completed 75 with a great curve ball. He could also run like a deer. When we did wind sprints he would come running by me backwards.

I found Cheraw, South Carolina, and, there on a wooden porch, sitting on a straight-back wooden chair tilted against the wall, was a man with a badge. I asked him, "Got any idea where Tom Brewer lives?" "Well...," (he took his sweet time looking me over and said,) "You must mean Austin! His daddy's name is Tom."

That afternoon we fished for crappie and caught two buckets full, which turned out to be barely enough when Tom ate 23 and I got rid of 18 of the deep fried beauties at his backyard party with friends. Friends? Everyone in town was a friend! Next morning, he got his beagles out and let them run for rabbits. How a dog with those short legs can run all day is beyond me, and he somehow had control of them with whistles and yells. Back at the house I was even served a drink over the shower door. No wonder Tom was always thinking of home.

The next day we went bird hunting with three of his friends. Quail in Southern California, where I grew up, were fairly big and had a prominent topnotch and used flying as a last ditch method, much preferring to run. So, there I was, looking for something that wasn't there when all of a sudden, with the noise of a helicopter gone mad, this teeny tiny bird scared the hell out of me and I simply pulled up the nose of the shotgun, one-handed and pulled the trigger in a purely gut reaction that made the sky look like a pillow blew up. Tom and the three guys gave me a strange look and I never got another first shot in all morning.

Toward dusk, Tom started calling in doves and, sure enough, the doves started cooing back. Wow! I could do it all over again without a gun and be thrilled.

For a number of years, Tom and I led the Red Sox pitching staff in victories, but never once was there a thread of jealousy. I can remember him yelling at me from the dugout to drag my right foot (to keep the ball down) and I used to holler at him to stay on top of the ball (making his curve better).

Sadly, 6,000 miles and 40 some years has made us strangers.

Tom Brewer

Kansas City and the Roundup

It was 1957 and I had just finished warming up for a game against Kansas City in their park. On my way to the dugout I heard a guy holler, "Hey Sully, you sad-son-of-a-bitch, what in hell are you doing here?" What am I doing here? I couldn't resist looking over into the box seats and saw a familiar face with a cowboy hat on. It was Chuck Williams. So I stopped and went over to the box which was far from my usual practice. Damn it was him, and I couldn't help but flash back on our many laughs in basic training at Camp Roberts in California. He and I shook hands and I told him I was there to provide for his *#*@%^! amusement.

As I went into the dugout to get ready for the game, I thought about a rainy night in 1951 standing at "Attention" on the pavement in front of our barracks at 3:00 AM. Our drill sergeants had gone somewhere and got totally drunk and now had decided to call out the troops for close order drill with steel helmets and M1 rifles and whatever we were wearing to bed that night. As we stood half-naked, Williams shouted out, "Sergeant! May I speak?" It took a moment for the dazed sergeant to find who had spoken. My thought was, "I hope he doesn't think I said that." "May I speak Sergeant?" Williams said again and the groan emitted by the guys around me was audible. Surprisingly, the sergeant said, "Yes, asshole, you may speak but it better be real good." "Sergeant, I believe we are about to march without a dress code." To which the sergeant replied, "And what code do you suggest fool?" "I suggest we all get NAKED!" The staggering sergeant then replied, "The fool is right! Drop 'em!" We went marching by the other barracks singing out in cadence that ugly morning with everything swinging!

Back to the day at hand. I pitched 9 innings and won easily. After, we met, had a few beers and I stayed all night at his cattle ranch a good distance from town.

Next morning he asked if I'd like to ride along as they moved some cows to another pasture. "Sure, if you have a saddle with long enough stirrups." He didn't and I must have looked like a jockey, but off we rode. These were small cutting horses and they know what they are out there to do and when mine all of a sudden caught sight of a stray, he immediately went into a lope to head the stray back, and then the cow bolted. Now we were in a full gallop. I was managing pretty good; in fact, I was starting to enjoy the whole thing with my eyes glued on the cow, when that beast got wide eyed and in full run, jumped a very deep ditch. I could see the headlines. "Red Sox pitcher wins 6 to 1 and is then killed while rounding up cattle!" My horse made the ditch and somehow I managed to stay on without having my voice change. It was then I decided my home is not on the range!

Shark River

My parents, Olive and Leal, and my mom's sister, Evelyn and her husband, Leroy, left California and arrived at the United Boat Works in Miami Beach. It was 1957 and I was taking them sailing with me on my 38' ketch the Mystery. We had no agenda other than pleasure. None of them had ever been sailing before and were as excited as kids as we left Biscayne Bay and went by Key Largo on our way to Marathon in the Florida Keys. I reduced the rig to just a big jib and the mizzen so the handling would be easy and turned off the motor. We sailed down the narrow waterway in no more than a 10 mile an hour breeze. Believe me, it was perfect and their excitement and enjoyment were so genuine that it was infectious.

After leaving Marathon a couple of days later, we headed due north toward Cape Sable which is the southern-most part of the Florida peninsula and the bottom of the Everglades. Upon sighting the shore we headed up the west side of the cape about 5 miles or so until we saw Ponce de Leon Bay. Just to the north the entrance to Shark River was masked by the mangrove bushes and trees, but I was bound to enter and with all the groundings I had been through, I felt confident I could get us free. We stopped offshore and I explained the risk and told them what I had read about the area and that I thought the reward was greater than the risk and they bought it. I got on the bowsprit and called back headings to my dad at the wheel. He responded with a superb job of just looking at the compass and steering to the number I called out. The secret is, in clear water, you have to stay in the darker colors, no matter what the channel seems to be.

Then, just like that, we were in amongst the 40' trees and foliage of the Everglades' lower delta. It is magical! The bottom is granite and all else floats or holds on to make a maze of waterways that is enchanting, to say the least. Again, there were no aids to navigation or detailed charts, so I kept track of all the turns as we slowly moved deeper into the interior. Spellbound is the best word. We were alone in the wilderness on a 38' boat and it was utopia! We anchored in 15' of clear clean water and I swam down to make sure the anchor was lodged in the granite. No mean feat when you think of the critters that live there. It was about 4:00 PM and we were tired from the long trip and the tension of getting into that remote estuary had been draining. I suggested early cocktails and it was gladly received. It was pure heaven, sitting there in the fading light listening to the start up of a night of wild sounds secure in our trusted floating home, when out of nowhere came a U.S. Marine Panther Jet Fighter that had to pull up slightly to miss our 46' mast. Next morning's laundry hanging on the railings was a bit larger than normal.

Leo Kiely

Leo Kiely was a left-hand relief pitcher from Hoboken, New Jersey, and played for the Boston Red Sox from 1951 to 1959 with two years out for Army duty. He was 6' 2" tall and only weighed 170 pounds which masked the fact that he was one of the all-time beer drinkers within my memory. Never loud, never out of hand, he could sit quietly in a bar or any other damn place and drink you into oblivion. I continually marveled at the way he would pour each bottle of beer slowly and deliberately into a small glass and savor each sip as if it were the first of the day. I believe he was made up of 98% liquid. After five warm up pitches he would literally be dripping sweat from the bill of his cap. His personality was as even keeled as anyone I had ever met and he had absolutely no enemies. I counted him as one of my best pals on the team. Leo and I had a standing order at the Midnight Pass Fishing Camp on Siesta Key in Sarasota, Florida, during spring training with the Red Sox that read as follows: Ice a case of Budweiser, put four dozen live shrimp in the bait well and have two sandwiches for our arrival the moment the daily workout ended which rarely went past noon. You didn't think the manager and coaches wanted to miss their starting times on the golf course?

I first met Leo in 1949 at Ocala, Florida, while spring training with the Birmingham Barons of the AA Southern Association. He made the team and I didn't. I was sent back to San Jose, California, and C ball. The next meeting was at Camp Drake outside Tokyo, Japan in December of 1952. I was in a group of guys walking back to our overnight barracks as we were leaving for San Francisco in the early A.M. and I saw a really fat body with Leo's head on it leading a group of soldiers marching down the street. I kept looking and as they got abreast of us I said, "Hey! Is that you Leo?" "Yeah, who wants to know?" He halted his troops, looked over and said, "Hey! Sully how the hell are you?" "None of your $%+&@#% business," I replied, "and how the hell you get so fat?" "The goddamn rice beer is blowing me up." We both laughed and hugged and stood there talking until his troops started grumbling. "See you back in the real world Sully. We'll play some ball and have some real beer."

Well, we did both, and later I am rooming with Leo in Kansas City in the Muelbach Hotel and after the game was over we went back to our room. Leo says, "let's get some beer up here, I'll split a case with ya" and he called room service to send up 24 bottles. I shook my head and said to him, "Sorry pal, I can't drink tonight because I'm pitching tomorrow." "Damn Sully I forgot." So Leo called room service back and told them to only send up 16.

Mickey Owen and Leo Kiely in the tunnel from the clubhouse to the dugout at Fenway Park.

Ted Williams the Carpenter

In 1957 the best baseball hitter of all time said, "We have a job to do this morning." "We?" I said, "What is this we stuff?"

I had made the sail from Boston to Florida and, despite many scary moments, I had docked in the marina at Islamorada the day before and had called Ted. He came down and picked me up and we had a lot of laughs as I related my trip experience. (He had said I would never make it.) But this morning he was back at the dock telling me to get in his car and we were going to the lumber yard to pick up a board. "Bush," he said, "we are going to install some shelves in the back of my carport!" OK, since he was going to take me bone fishing the next day, it was hard to turn down the "we" stuff. But believe me I knew after spending four years with the man at that point "we" meant I was to blame if anything went wrong.

It did from the very beginning. Ted Williams did not own a tape measure! I said, "Hey # 9, where is the tape measure?" "Don't need one Bush, just be ready to cut where I say." I gave him my best Buster Keaton look of stupidity and waded into a most difficult few hours. "Goddamit, Bush, I told you to cut the *%#^$@ board here!" "And that's where I cut the *%^$#& thing!" I'd argue to a deaf ear. He would walk up to the wall and extend his right hand to the door jamb and his left hand to the wall and then hold them (he thought) that far apart walking back to the board where I waited with saw in hand. He would then bend over putting his left hand on the end of the board and when his right hand touched down he would say, "There, cut it there! God Almighty Sullivan! Can't you get it right just once?"

After wasting the entire board, we made our second trip to the lumber yard in silence to get another 1x12x16 clear pine board. As the lumberman was putting a red flag on the end of the board sticking out of the back seat of Ted's Cadillac convertible I asked him if he had done this before. He said, "Great hitter, terrible carpenter."

I reflected on that as I retreated from his house to my boat after installing the worst looking shelving I have ever seen or been part of. Ted's final words to me that day were, "Jesus Christ, Bush, I can only hope you fish better than you cut wood. "Yeah," I said, "and I know you can fish better than you measure." He laughed and said he'd see me early.

It was black when he picked me up the next morning with boat in tow. Upon arriving at the launch ramp just as the sun broke over the horizon, I jumped out of the car looking to buy a case of beer. I didn't get halfway across the yard before he had the boat in the water and the engine running. He yelled, "Get your ass over here Bush or I'm fishing alone." Damn! I thought, how the hell can you fish without beer? But fish without beer we did and spent the whole day doing it too. Ted poled the boat all day long on the flats as we searched for the bone fish. I never saw one before

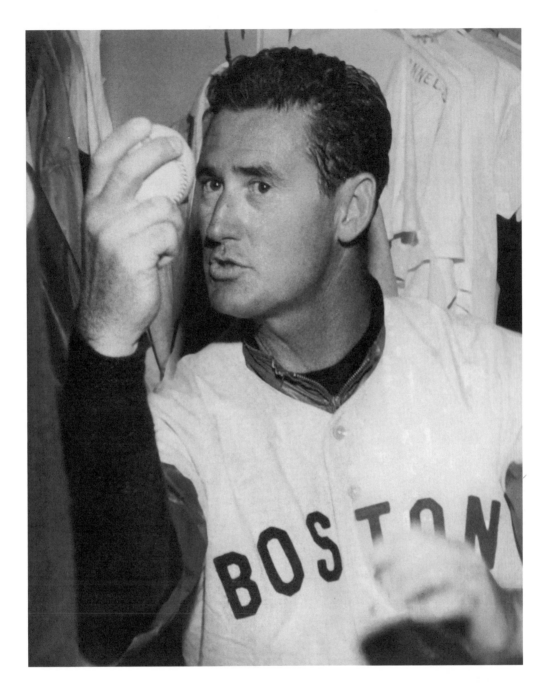

he did. His concentration was unreal and he was strict as hell about me keeping the rod tip in the same direction as my eyes so there would be no wasted motion the minute we saw a fish. Thank God I caught the first fish we saw which made the day easier, but Ted worked every minute we were out there and I have never been more exhausted after a day of fishing.

But just think, I spent eight years watching the best hitter and got to fish a day with the best fisherman, but I also spent a couple of hours with the worst carpenter.

Characters

From time to time in everyday life, you hear of a person being labeled a character. Baseball has always been filled with them. For instance, when I played in Oroville, California. Jules Hudson, a left-handed pitcher and one of the first "bonus babies," took me deer hunting wearing a suit and tie. Later that year he had all his teeth pulled because he had always wanted false teeth. The last I heard of him, he was in the Eastern League and when he got in trouble in a game he would take his dentures out, put them in his back pocket and then grin at the batter.

While trying to make a living, a lot of the Globe Trotters basketball players played other sports. Once in the minor leagues when I was playing for Scranton, Pennsylvania, I got a base hit. When I got to first base where "Sweet Water" Clifton was playing and before the next pitch I asked, "How you doing Sweet?" He looked at me and said, "I ain't going to tell you. I'm a busy man."

Hershel Freeman was a tall, thick, hard throwing right hander from Gadsden, Alabama. We roomed together in Scranton and every morning, and I mean every morning, he would come in my room and wake me up and ask, "What are we doing today, roomie?" Every morning I would explain to him that there was nothing to do and therefore waking me up was about to ruin our relationship. But every morning I roomed with him I never got to sleep in.

In 1957, Clint Courtney was catching for the Washington Senators and after a game in their park he noticed me looking for a cab to the train station as I had missed the team bus. He offered me a ride to the train station which I accepted as we had been teammates in Mexico. We walked across the hot parking lot to a four-door Cadillac. As Clint opened the driver's door and got in to release the lock for the passenger side, I got the first whiff of the interior. Words can't do it justice. It was overwhelming and from one moment standing next to a beautiful white "Caddie," the next moment I was reduced to not wanting to enter this skid row bar. Clint said, "Come on, let's go!" Understand, in my time, ball players were a clannish breed and to ignore or refuse was to risk indelible harm to that association and, while walking away from this made great sense, there was still the train to catch. On the way to the station the dialog went like this: "Nice car, Clint." "Yeah, I get a new one every year I stay in the big leagues." "Ever thought of getting rid of all those beer cans in the back seat?" "Naw, the baseball season will be over soon and I'll be trading this in." "How many beer cans you think might be back there?" "What's six times the number of home games we've played?"

Since I was the tallest pitcher in the American League then, I had to suffer through a lot of tall and short photo shots. Here I am with Washington's Albie Pearson at Griffith Stadium. At least I have more bats than he does!"

Traded to the Phillies

I bought a home in Fort Lauderdale, Florida. I invited my parents to live there and they suffered my comings and goings like the troopers they were. In the winter of 1960, I was home briefly prior to sailing to Nassau. I was on one of the commercial docks just inside the main channel to the Atlantic Ocean at Fort Lauderdale. One of the longshoremen loading the 195′ freighter I was checking cargo on, prior to our departure the next day, called me to the phone. I picked it up and a telegraph operator said, "I have a telegram for you from the Red Sox that reads as follows: YOU HAVE BEEN TRADED TO THE PHILLIES, GOOD LUCK." I remember saying to her, "honest?" I was destroyed. I stood there with the receiver in my hand and felt my heart trying to get out of my chest cavity. After eight years in the Majors and five in the Minors all with the Boston Red Sox, that telegram was all there was. Not even the decency to call me in person. I won't bore you with loyalty, pitching hurt, and basic courtesy.

I made a call to George Page in Boston, whom I considered my second father. George was the reason I was traveling with the freighter. He had some large dollars tied up in the operation and asked me to go aboard and find out what was going on. George said, "Okay, that's the way life goes and the key is to make a positive out of it. How much did the Sox pay you?" "I started at $6,000 and was up to $21,000." George couldn't believe it and said, "Okay, when the Phillies call, tell them you are not sure if you want to play any more because you can make more money with me." I was shocked for the second time in that day. "Jesus, George, I'm not sure I want to do that." "Trust me, they would not have traded for you if they didn't want you. Just tell them that."

Sure enough, Gene Mauch (Phillies manager and teammate in 1956-57) called the house that evening and I took the call in the kitchen where my mom was cooking dinner. "Great to have you aboard Frank, I can sure use you." "Gene, I really appreciate your trust but I think I'm going to call it quits and keep working here." I thought my mom was going to faint! "What's the problem Frank?" "I'll be honest with you Gene, it isn't worth it to me unless I get some more money." "How much you need Sully?" It was then that I realized I was totally unprepared for that moment and stammered out the largest figure I could think of. "$25,000 Gene." He then replied, "That's easy Sully. You got it."

For the second time that day I stood with a receiver in my hand, but this time wanting to kill myself. Then again, agents were unheard of in those days.

Now you know why most players have them.

It Takes Talent to Lose 107

If baseball wants to be the game for the new millennium, they need to let the pitchers in Denver use Nerf balls. Thin air lets the ball travel too far and there is not enough resistance to make a spinning ball break enough.

When I was traded to the Phillies (I still shudder when I think of that team), we played Pittsburgh in an exhibition game there in the spring of 1961. The charter plane (Lockheed Electra) landed in the snow, thankfully at the airport. A big Greyhound-like bus came out to the plane to pick us up. After we all got seated, the driver put it in gear and we didn't move. We just sat there with the wheels spinning. I kid you not, we all got out and pushed that big bastard to get it rolling and, one at a time, we hopped in the open door. It takes a long time to get 35 guys in a bus if it isn't moving. If it is moving, the last guy in has to run at least a half mile! It was the best work out we had all year. I know it was one of the only things we did good together.

We went to the park as a mere formality, never thinking we would have to play the game because it was so cold. We were shocked to see 6,000 people sitting in the snow. Nothing to do but play the thing, so both teams got together with the umpires and decided not to throw any breaking balls and anything caught was a strike. They beat us 2 to 1 and we were out of there in an hour and fifty-five minutes. Bob Skinner hit a ball off me that I just missed catching. The damn thing went out of the park like a shot!

That team was so bad we used to have victory parties on rain-out days. We were led by Gene Mauch (manager) who everyone but his players thought was a genius. He kept managing for one run while we were getting beat by ten. Prior to losing 23 games in a row, which was a new National League record, we lost 11 games in a row, only to win one and screw up an unbeatable record. It was after the 23rd loss as we disembarked from a plane in Philadelphia, that I cautioned all the players to stay 5 yards apart so one artillery shell wouldn't get us all. We lost 107 games! Our best hitter, Tony Gonzalez, hit 277. Robin Roberts was 1-10 and he is in the Hall of Fame. I was 3-16. I found it hard to pitch with tears in my eyes. It all seemed (for me) to come to a bitter end when Mauch didn't reimburse my fine ($75) for intentionally hitting Frank Thomas of the Mets in a game in New York when he ordered it done!

The biggest surprise of that whole experience was the reaction of the baseball fans of that city. Their reputation for booing Santa Claus was documented but with us they could see it would be a waste of time.

My biggest fan and best pal before a game at Fenway Park, my dad Leal Sullivan.

Let's Go for a Swim!

George Page called me at my home in Fort Lauderdale and said, "Take the boat to Coral Harbor and I will meet you there in a week." Coral Harbor is on the south side of New Providence Island in the Bahamas. I took my parents along as crew and we delivered his 55' Chris-Craft unscathed to that resort's fine marina.

The trouble all started on the practice putting green in front of the resort clubhouse. My dad, Leal, and I were unmercifully pestered by this cute waitress into ordering a couple of rum concoctions that had enough alcohol in them to keep the battleship Missouri at sea for a month.

After making a winning putt, Dad thought another of those "Rum Blasters" was in order. I agreed and the waitress hurried back with the lethal "whammers." I think mine came with the little paper umbrella singed.

We had promised my mother, Olive, that we would join her poolside, but she hadn't come off the boat yet so there was time for one more game. Again, my father was victorious and he thought one more "TNT in a glass" should fill the bill. This time I think my pineapple was charred.

To say that Dad and I were feeling no pain as we dropped into lounge chairs beside Mom at the deep end of the pool is simply a waste of time. She took one look at her two guys with the silly grins and wished she was somewhere else.

As we sat by the pool watching people using the one meter diving board, I was talking with Mom about something when I noticed my dad calmly get up out of his lounge chair and stride to the back of the diving board. He smiled easily as he stepped up on it and was nonchalant as anyone I had ever seen as he tested the bend of the board. He then returned to the back of the board and, honestly, I was impressed as he took two strides forward and lifted into the air then came down depressing the board perfectly. It sprang back up propelling him high in the air and he performed a hell of a nice dive, headfirst into the pool. I said to my mother, "Jesus, Mom, that was unbelievably good!" She said, "That may be, Frank, but you had better go get the damn fool, because he doesn't know how to swim."

I bolted from my chair and went into the water, not bothering to take off my sun glasses, hat, slippers, shirt, etc. It was all for naught as my father came to the surface doing some never seen before side-stroke method he had just invented and made it to the edge of the pool smiling like a Cheshire cat.

Whenever the three of us would recount that afternoon, we'd get tears in our eyes from laughing. Now, with both of them gone, I just get tears in my eyes.

Things I Remember

It was impossible, when I recently saw a game in Fenway Park, to bring up in my memory a clear picture of being on the mound for 9 innings in any particular game. Sure, there are small indelible moments, but of the 73 complete games I threw, not one remains fully there in my brain. Some parts of games do though.

The day I pitched 9 innings and won in Kansas City the temperature was well over 110 on the field and I lost 13 pounds while having to walk off the mound onto the grass after every pitch because my baseball spikes were so hot. All my infielders were doing the same in their area. I had to change shirts every inning and wound up the game in one of Ted Williams' uniforms.

A home run Billy Martin hit off me in Fenway Park so incensed Higgins (manager) that he didn't talk to me for two weeks. Brash Billy would come to the top of the Red Sox dugout at the start of every season and call out to Higgins, "Hey Pinky! How many World Series tickets you want me to try and get for you?"

I got a hit off Herb Score and heard his catcher, Jim Hegan, yell, "Oh! No!"

I pitched 9 innings and won the last game of the season in a game that beat out Detroit for 4th place to help out everyone's off season income. I was sitting in the 110 degree whirlpool when a glass of brandy arrived from Tom Yawkey (owner). Stupid here drank the thing like it was a beer and could hardly get out of the now "death pool" and walked on rubber legs for hours.

My very first starting assignment was in Yankee Stadium and I struck out Mantle three times in a row. When he came to the plate for the fourth and last time I was leading 6 to 0 and was wondering why he got all the press. His next swing made it 6 to 3 and I can remember thinking, "Now I know."

In one game I slid into third base after hitting a ball off the wall and our third base coach, Jack Burns, helped me up and extended his hand saying, "Let me introduce myself, you have never been here before."

A game in Chicago when Billy Pierce (White Sox) and I got a new ball every pitch as the game started and ended in pouring rain. He had a high leg kick and I didn't and I thought he'd be in trouble in the mud. I was the one who struggled.

Ted Williams coming out of left field and yelling at me about a pitch I threw and I told him he ought to worry about catching something out where he was playing. I was immediately sorry I had said it but he took it and continued to treat me well.

Top: Billy Goodman is on the left. Norm Zauchin is covering the bag but I take care of "The Scooter" myself. Phil Rizzuto! You are tagged out!

Bottom: I stood up after being called safe at third with my only triple and Jack Burns (third base coach) came over and put out his hand saying, "I'd like to introduce myself because you have never been here before."

REFLECTIONS ON THE GAME

Just Joking

At times, I have been asked to relate some of my experiences while pitching in the Major Leagues. Frankly, I have been reluctant to do so as the game, in my opinion, is flawed. There are far too many hitters. Why did someone make up a game with so many damn hitters? When I pitched there seemed to be a never ending stream of hitters crawling out of the other team's dugout. It was as if someone had knocked the top off an ant hill! I remember standing on the mound during a particularly bad outing and thinking, "If I could shut off the opening to that dugout, I wouldn't be making such a fool out of myself."

At any rate, for those of you interested in becoming a pitcher, I have compiled a list of what I remember is good and what I remember is bad while pitching.

It **is** good:

...if the batter is arguing with the umpire.

...if the catcher has his mask off looking straight up.

...if the batter is walking back to the dugout yelling things about your mother.

...if the manager shakes your hand after the game.

It **is not** good:

...if people in your home park start leaving when your name is announced.

...if the hitter turns left after running to first base.

...if you keep seeing the big numbers on the outfielder's uniforms.

...if everyone is looking into the bleachers after the batter hits the ball.

...if the scoreboard is running out of numbers behind the other team's name.

...if you are showering alone before the game is over.

Other known facts:

It is 60 feet six inches from the pitching rubber to home plate, which is too far when throwing the ball, but not far enough if it is hit!

Some fool, way back when, decided that pitchers needed to run wind sprints constantly all season long to keep their arms strong. This, in the face of the fact that the great sprinter Carl Lewis never won a single baseball game!

There has never been a baseball field with a fence high enough.

TV cameramen are trained to catch ball players spitting and adjusting their jockstraps.

If someone **today** were to make up a game where you try to hit a round ball with a round bat, they would be put away.

Finally, baseball is the way society keeps people off the streets who are not capable of holding a real job.

This photo, taken in our Sarasota, Florida, spring training club house, pretty much shows the relationship I had with Manager Mike Higgins. Looking back on it now I would describe the relationship as being difficult for the both of us. Not hostile by any means, but not as easy as it should or could have been. I wish now we had sat down at some point and talked it all out.

Baseball Basics

I have been asked, from time to time, to explain the game of baseball or at least shed some light on how it is played and why. Let's get something straight right now. No one knows why! But let's start at the "Big Inning." (Sorry...)

Let's see, Jesus was catching for the Red Sea Raiders in the Ten Commandment League when baseball first came on the scene. Hey! Hold it! Calm down. I'm just joking. I know he played second base.

At that time, baseball was played by the sundial which was distressing because on cloudy days they didn't know when to quit. So, it was decided or perhaps deemed, that the game would be over at dusk because head lamps weren't invented yet. Then Moses (the designated hitter) said that an inning would be three outs for each team. Why Moses? Well, after what he had just pulled off at the Red Sea who was going to knock an inning? Why nine innings? How do I know? I was born in 1930! The main thing here was to get the damn game over before it got dark and the lions started to roam around.

All this lasted until they decided to put lights in Wrigley Field, much to the consternation of the people in that Chicago neighborhood. They felt sleep was needed to be able to fetch the newspapers in the morning to find out who had won the Cubs game the night before. Is anyone with me?

The reason I bring all this up is to try and explain to those of you who are not satisfied with a mere statement and need clarification of facts that should accompany such statements, that I am not the one qualified to do it. Look! I know my limits! I am best qualified to drink and criticize someone else.

So, where are we? Oh, yeah, you need answers. Let's just say that a game that requires a round ball to be hit by a round bat is, even in this modern day when we don't hand crank autos to get them started, ludicrous! Who thought of all this 90 feet between bases stuff? Who made a pitcher's mound 60 feet six inches from home plate. Who thought of the term home plate? Give me a break! You have to touch home plate after you have hit a home run? Rational people, never introduced to baseball terminology at an early age, might as well go to a soccer game and wonder why they don't put the team names on the uniforms.

At any rate, it is a sad day that I have to spend all this time and effort to try and explain the National Pastime to people who are already overwhelmed with all the free information they are getting from their computers. How can anyone think about the game when they can get information about how to save a whale despite the over abundance of the damn things and starving people?

Tommy Dorsey and the Ground Keepers

Tommy Dorsey was a baseball fanatic and a Boston Red Sox fan. If the Dorsey Band was playing anywhere near where the Red Sox were, there was an open invitation to join him when the game was over. The Dorsey Band bus would be waiting in front of the team hotel and a player could opt to get on his bus and go to places like the Palladium Theater in New York, where one night, as Tommy's guest, I sat next to Joe DiMaggio and listened to Sinatra sing with the band. Or the Meadow Brook nightclub in New Jersey and have dinner on Tommy and enjoy the unbelievable ambiance. He would always come to the table after playing a set and make you feel like a king. He knew baseball and his questions were about trying to understand the game better. I'm not sure he was talking to the right people. Hell, I have never seen a baseball rule book. In fact, I have never known anybody who had one. Maybe that's why most of us who played the game might be accused of fooling with the rules from time to time. Not knowing the rules, you can understand my horror now to find out that "quick" pitching was not allowed. So, it is with great reluctance that I tell you there may have been a few batters not completely ready in the batter's box who looked up to find a sizzling fastball already on the way toward them. Surely, if I had known what I do now, I would have waited patiently for the poor batter to completely get set and dug in. Surely.

Ah, but the worst manipulators of rules were the ground keepers. The biggest culprits were in Cleveland and Chicago. The Chicago White Sox of the mid-fifties were a speedy team who bunted a lot and their ground crew chief made the base paths at Comiskey Park hard and fast and blatantly tilted the third base foul line toward the field so that any ball rolling along the line would stay fair. To add to that, he let the grass grow higher out in front of home plate and put enough water in that area that made it impossible for a pitcher to pick up the bunt and set his feet to throw. Despite a dry summer, it was like trying to make a play in a swamp.

On the other hand, the Cleveland Indians had a team made up of older, slower players and a batter could not bunt a ball fair down the third base line because it was tilted foul by their grounds crew. The infield grass was cut high to slow the ball down and the base paths were almost plowed to prevent base stealing.

Both ballparks had pitching mounds tailored for their staffs. At the time, I was the tallest pitcher in the American League, therefore, my stride when throwing was the longest. It seemed more than a mere coincidence in those cities that my left foot, the one that all the weight comes down on, found only loose soil and uneven landing places. Can you believe it? I just found out that the ground crew chiefs in those cities were the Brossard brothers.

LIFE IS MORE THAN 9 INNINGS

Awe Inspiring

After playing professional baseball for more than 16 years, I consider myself a good judge of what is pretty good in that game.

I watched teammate Ted Williams for eight seasons and was still shocked when he said he could tell if he hit one seam or two seams of the ball that was coming his way at nearly 100 mph. We called him on it and he put pine tar on the head of his bat to mark the ball when it was struck and called 9 out of 10 right. Another time, during a game at Fenway Park and with Bob Lemon pitching for Cleveland, he tried to scare a loudmouth fan yelling at him from a box seat behind first base with foul balls off his bat. He hit five pitches into that box. It was unbelievable and Lemon, a great pitcher, could only shake his head.

I saw Satchel Page in Knoxville led to the mound blindfolded and left alone after being spun around, throw eight of ten strikes to a catcher at home plate.

The best fights in baseball were on Saturday afternoon games in Fenway Park. Promoters would bring truck drivers up from Providence, R.I. in buses stocked with cold beer. They always made the mistake of getting them to Boston a little too early before the game and these gentlemen would take full advantage of the many pubs close by the park. Many times we simply stopped the game to watch.

All the above stand out and are rated high, but folks, the all-time number ONE feat was managed during a National League game in Candlestick Park, San Francisco. In the 6th inning, Willie Mays swung so hard at a ball thrown by Dallas Green of the Phillies that his teammates feared a hernia. The ball was hit straight up and almost out of sight with incredible backspin which took it over the Philly dugout and above the seats in the stands.

The scene shifts to a gentleman coming out of the tunnel that leads to the concessions. He is walking in the aisle toward his box seat with a hot dog in one hand and a large paper cup of beer in the other. Unaware what has happened, he is momentarily at a loss why all the people are pointing and looking up. Then he spots the ball and, without breaking stride or changing pace, he shoves the hot dog wrapped in wax paper into his mouth, reaches up with that hand, catches the ball, puts it in his pocket, pulls the hot dog out of his mouth and walks calmly forward to a standing ovation without spilling a single drop of beer. The game came to an understandable halt as players, who to a man, can't stand the sight of spilled beer, tipped their caps to the gentleman. He responded to players and crowd by raising the cup of beer and downing it in one majestic swig.

Grown men wept!

Opposite: Ted Williams in 1954 – autographed "to a great kid."

Needing an Agent

Once I did a Gillette ad for television and think I got paid $300.00 but had to pay the cab ride to and from the studio while in New York.

In 1954, Dom DiMaggio asked me to have my picture taken with a king-sized mattress in a Red Sox uniform to tout his company's product. I was flattered and did it as a favor.

I also remember making $500.00 to be at the opening of the Key West, Florida, dog track. I was there (by sailing my boat alone from Miami) to present the trophies to each winning owner. It was built by dredging out a deep lake and depositing the resulting sand all around it making the dog track. At the opening, one of the greyhounds jumped the railing and wound up in the lake and a trainer went into the lake to save the dog, but damned near drowned himself when the dog climbed all over him in panic.

Anyway, this was in the days when companies like Topps Bubble Gum gave us either $250.00 cash or merchandise each year to put our mugs on their baseball cards. Most of us took the goods that Topps offered and were happy that they were worth more than the cash. Things like furniture, electronics, appliances, etc. And believe me, we needed them to help relieve the suffering in the rental homes we could afford in the towns we played for in those days.

But the best was when Willard Nixon called me one afternoon in Chicago (I think it was 1954) and said, "Hey Sully, Tom Brewer and I are going out to Dubow Sporting Goods. Wanna come? They are going to give each of us a set of golf clubs, a golf bag and a pull cart for signing with them." "No kidding?" I said. "Don't leave without me."

We piled into a cab and went out to the factory and were totally impressed by the treatment we got. We then eagerly signed on the dotted line to represent their company for LIFE! We also split the two-way cab fare three ways.

I have to add, the only "Frank Sullivan" baseball glove made by Dubow I have ever seen (a wretched looking piece of leather and stuffing) was here on Kauai. I was embarrassed to sign it for the kid but youth needs to be served. (Now there is an arguable point!)

At any rate, I think it is only fitting that one year after signing with Dubow, while I was having my best season, Wilson Sporting Goods offered me $10,000.00 (more than half of what I was making with the Red Sox at the time) to sign with them, but because I had already signed a lifetime contract...

Hey? Why would a smart guy like me need an agent?

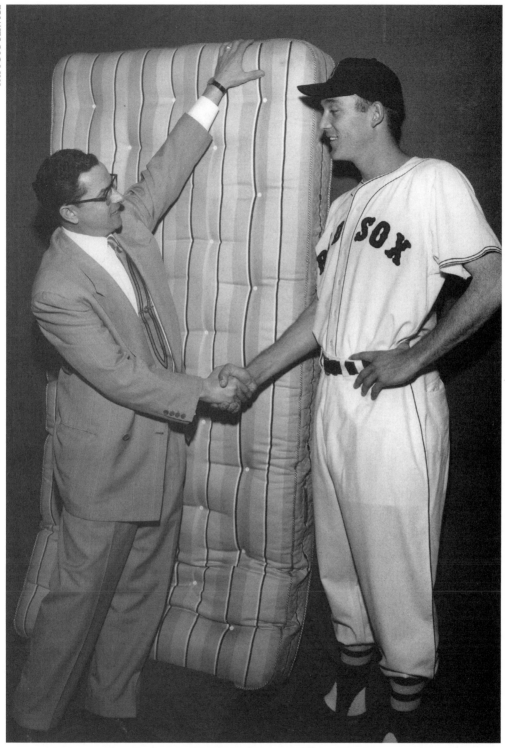

Dom DiMaggio had just retired and owned a mattress company. He was touting one of the first king-size mattresses and wanted me to promote it. I did it for nothing just so I could get to meet him. It was worth it as he is a wonderful man.

The Makings of a Good Pitcher

The best way for a pitcher to arrive in the Major Leagues is (like I did) to be unknown. He will have a tremendous advantage over batters who haven't seen him before and they will have to adjust to his throwing arm angle and motion. Then it is still awhile before they start zeroing in on his preferences when he gets in trouble and put in a bad "pitch count," like two balls and no strikes, or three balls and no strikes, or three balls and one strike. Good hitters think. It is really unfortunate.

This brings us (in some way?) to the making of a good pitcher. First he has to have a good "arm." Meaning, he is able to "hum it." Second, he has to be able to throw a strike when he has to. Maybe in Rangoon all pitchers are ready-made and it's just unfortunate that they don't play baseball there, but for the rest of the world, throwers become pitchers only when they finally understand the problem. For me, it happened in a game in Albany, New York, in the Class A Eastern League. Len Okrie, my catcher, came out on the pitching mound and simply said, "Stop worrying about what you are doing out here and start worrying about what is happening at home plate." It was as if a light went ON! It was just like throwing rocks again and, believe me, I was the best rock thrower in my neighborhood... period!

Let me put it this way, if an unknown pitcher comes up to the "big show" from the low minor leagues and can "bring it" to the plate above the 90 mph number, with control, he has a good chance of staying longer than the reputed "cup of coffee." And if the ball he throws has "something on it" and is moving unpredictably when it gets over the hitting area, the batters will really have to pay attention to this guy. He, in turn, will do just fine if he will adjust to what will be happening to him. Like the opposing team will start an intense study of why he is successful and will start picking his delivery apart. The coaches will start a systematic scan of his throwing motion to see if there is any tip off to what is coming so they can alert the hitter by yelling things like "heads up" or "look out" for a breaking ball and "nail it" or "jump on it" for a fastball. It never ends either! They are always picking and prying. The bastards won't leave well enough alone!

Add the fact that good hitters have memories like elephants and if they face a pitcher anytime in their life, they will remember every pitch and immediately spread the word around the league faster than a lady's bridge game conversation. I say let's make the decision that should have been made long ago. The decision that will right baseball forever. I say BAN LADIES BRIDGE GAMES!

I took Mel Parnell's place in the starting pitcher rotation in 1954 when Mickey McDermott broke Mel's arm pitching to him in Washington.

Mel never once said a bad thing or did anything but support me from then on. He remains a dear friend. Later when he got healthy again he took someone else's spot and continued his great career. I watched him throw a no-hit game in Fenway Park considered to be impossible by a left-hand pitcher.

Hitting Frank Thomas

Question: How can a guy throw a ball through a small rectangle that is 60'6" away when the rectangle is only as large as an umpire wants it to be and from umpire to umpire isn't in the same place?

Answer: It can only be done with concentration that might amaze the non-athletic public, but surprisingly it eludes most of the pitchers who gain the coveted Major League status and, therefore, failure is guaranteed. No matter how you get there, if you want to stay at that level as a pitcher, you have to be able to throw a strike that pleases the umpire for the day on demand. (Sounds like my house!)

Therefore, when the pitcher is asked to come out of all that zeroing in to hit or "brush" back a batter, it has two effects. One good and one bad. Satisfaction felt by the teammates for the retribution is the positive, but the downside is the loss of that precious mental zeroing-in. Think I'm wrong? Next time you see that sort of thing start, just watch what happens to the pitcher's control for the next few batters. It's like waking up in the middle of a beautiful dream. Damn!

I vividly remember the last man a manager ordered me to hit. It was Frank Thomas with the Mets in the Polo Grounds in New York. The year was 1961 and we were leading the game 7 to 3 with no reason in the world to hit the guy. Gene Mauch said do it and because I was a friend of Frank's, (I had played with him when we were both members of Frank Shea's All-Stars touring New England after the Major League season was over in 1956) I told Clay Dalrymple (catcher) to tell Frank to be "alive."

I threw the first pitch about waist high and about a foot inside. Frank, knowing I was going to throw at him stepped back and swung at it and missed, strike one! I assumed he didn't get the message and yelled at Clay, "He knows?" Clay nodded.

Next pitch I buzzed him further inside and Frank stepped further back and swung at it and missed! Now the umpire knows what is going on and Frank is smiling at me and Mauch is livid in the dugout. At this point I want to hit Thomas and do it with a fastball right in his chest. The ball rebounds out toward me and Frank runs out of the batter's box toward me, so for the instant I am not sure if I'm going to be involved in a fight or what. Frank, the silly bastard, stops and picks the ball up and gently tosses it to me underhanded and says, "If that's the best you got, Sully, it's time to get out of the game."

Sadly he was right. Little did I know that Addison's disease was rearing its ugly head and my stamina and adrenalin were suffering. I guarantee the reader that only a few years earlier Frank Thomas might have been dead with a hole in his chest.

Why is Baseball Different?

To me there has always been something about a baseball game that is different from all the other sports. Is it because the ballparks have different dimensions and the walls have different heights? Or is it because you don't have to sit riveted every second of the action for an extended period of time. People can have a decent conversation while watching a baseball game without losing the essence of either.

Maybe it's because each player seems to have a different way of approaching home plate with his bat in hand while every pitcher has his own style and motion and way of walking around the pitcher's mound. Surely it's not the lull between pitches is it? Is style the answer? Some players wear tight fitting uniforms and others look like they slept in them. Some players wear their pant's legs down and some wear them high and all the body types are represented in this sport that allows small men to compete with big men equally.

Here is a thought: maybe it's because the people in attendance get to keep the ball when it comes into the stands. Or does the color of each bat being different and of varying sizes have anything to do with it? Why are players thrown out by only a fraction of one step at first base almost every time?

Surely it's not the endless statistics that are ragged on by the announcers! I hope it's not because I would hate to think that any player "worth his salt" was ever on that page. Maybe it's a way of staying in the big city long enough to miss the traffic! No. That's wrong, 25,000 people leaving a game is traffic.

Could it be the hot dogs and beer or in this day and age the good food? Or is it because the game stops after a player hits a home run and everyone watches him slowly round and touch all the bases as if he might miss one? I hope it's not because you have to line up to get to a urinal between innings. Perhaps it's the heat of the summer in all those big cities driving people out of their homes to a ballpark where they can escape their concrete jungle for a few hours? No, not in this day of air-conditioning. Does the fact that there is no clock to end the games have anything to do with it? Then, because my memory is old, maybe all the above is only my imagination.

I bring this all up because the one thing I remember baseball differing greatly from all other sports was the fact that it used to be affordable for a hard-working father to take his family to a game without having to work overtime for the next three months to pay for it. In my mind, that is the problem the owners and players should address equally.

If I owned a team I would have a "standing room only" area and not charge for it during the regular season so anyone could come and go and have a peek and the truant officers would have a place to make their quota. That, and the parking lot guy could make a extra buck. Alright, alright, if I was the owner, I'd own the parking lot too.

LIFE IS MORE THAN 9 INNINGS

What It's Like for a Starting Pitcher

Game day, Fenway Park, Boston Red Sox vs. Chicago White Sox, Sullivan pitching for Boston, Wynn for Chicago.

Try and get breakfast down without thinking what is ahead for the day. Stay as quiet as possible on your way to the ballpark and above all don't get mad about anything as you're going to need all the adrenaline you can muster later.

Don't arrive at the clubhouse too early as the room will be warm and tend to sap your energy slightly, along with all the pre-game preparation and commotion. Put your sanitary socks on and pull the uniform socks over them. Step into jockey shorts and pull on your jockstrap. Snap in the protector and put on a light t-shirt. Go lie down on one of the training tables and control, control, control the adrenaline surge. If you're lucky, you may even nap.

It's Doc Fadden tapping your arm. OK Sully. You're on stage! OK, easy still. Walk over to your locker and put on the rest of the uniform then tie your spikes on real tight. Reach onto the top shelf of the locker and grab your glove with the ball that Manager Higgins gave you when you came in. It's twenty minutes before game time and now let the adrenaline start coming slowly until you enter the tunnel under the stands that leads to the dugout and then really let it out until the back of your neck is tingling. Remind yourself out loud you are not going out there to find out who is going to win. YOU are going to DOMINATE!

There is a smattering of applause from the early birds in the stands when they see you emerge from the dugout. Just nod but don't get involved. The warm-up mounds at Fenway are between the backstop and the dugouts and as you step up on the mound and start tossing the ball with the warm-up catcher, acknowledge Mrs. Yawkey (owner's wife) sitting in her sky box alone. When she sees you tip your hat, she will give a tiny wave with crossed fingers.

Throw only enough to get good and loose and just release one good fastball as there has never been a game won warming up. By all means do not even peek over at Early Wynn throwing only thirty yards away. That teddy bear of a man off the field is just about to explode and is looking for anything to get himself even madder. His own teammates wouldn't dare say anything to him now. If you were to even nod his way, he will knock you on your ass the first time you're at bat.

It's time, and you run on the field with the rest of the team and stride to the top of the pitching mound, pick up the resin bag and throw it down hard. You're ready and at this moment a bugler should blow CHARGE! Instead, you will have to stop everything, take your cap off and wait for the National Anthem to end.

Opposite: At my best.

Changes Against Pitchers

Every time I pick up the paper and get to the sports page there seems to be an article about the baseball being more lively these days. In essence the stories say that baseball games are starting to look like launch day at Cape Canaveral. Balls are leaving the confines in record numbers. The question posed by the sportswriters is why? WHY? Where the hell have they been? What the hell have they been looking at? Would they recognize a baseball game if they saw one? (OK, OK, I'll try and calm down.)

Let me remind the reader that the single factor in favor of the pitchers in the last 40 years is the favorable check swing calls by the first and third base umpires. Other than that one item, the guys who "toe the rubber" have systematically been relieved of every advantage they ever had.

First, they lowered the mound. Why? I'll tell you why! (I really do need to calm down.) The ranks of the sportswriter were growing in unbelievable numbers. Not men who studied and knew the game, but men with no interest and no patience who decided a 2-hit shutout was boring! So the press and TV ratings and a weak baseball commissioner took away the best angle of attack the pitchers had.

It used to be that pitchers were able to pitch with a ball that had been in play for a while. Not now! Now they throw out almost every ball that touches the ground. New baseballs are very hard to spin. (I'm getting upset again.)

Also, batters are crowding the plate in record numbers. They are allowed to go to the plate wearing enough armor to ward off gunfire. The umpires are ignoring the batter's box dimensions. If a pitcher throws inside trying to keep the hitter honest and back in the area he is supposed to be in by rule, he is ejected and fined and chastised by the press as a misfit and threat to society. (Now I am really hot.)

I say let them play the game like it used to be played. No batting helmets or pads or gloves and use the ball until they lose it. If they want to stop the rockets then let's go back to the days of Don Drysdale and Early Wynn. If those two had to pay a dollar for every brush back pitch they threw, they would have had to borrow money to eat. Let's go back to Sal "The Barber" Maglie who didn't get his nickname from cutting hair. All the hitters knew if they crowded the plate, Sal would give them a close shave.

Yes, if they want to get rid of the fireworks just give the pitchers back the tools. Take the armor off the hitters and get them back in the batter's box and let the pitchers keep them there. That will stop the rockets and the red glare too!

There, I feel better now.

Winning Baseball

May I suggest you have someone else get the hot dogs and drinks if you go to a baseball game. Try and concentrate on what is happening in front of you every moment of the time it takes to complete the game. Then again, maybe the time factor troubles those of you hellbent on having everything planned to the minute. After all, it is one of the only sports not regulated by a clock. (Horseshoes, darts, pitching coins, tetherball and Anne-Anne-over, are important others.)

I think the key to watching a game is to have an idea beforehand on the tendencies of the managers. One managerial theory is to let the horses run. Let the big hitters hit away and try to get the "big inning." Another game-plan is to try to steal a run with crafty players and make sure that defense is your big suit. Know, when you see a batter take a pitch right down the middle when he is ahead of the count, the manager probably put the take sign on. It's all being orchestrated in front of you by each manager.

I found winning all came down to the team managers who understood and knew what to do with the people they were dealt by the general managers. Each player has an individual talent the manager has to weave into the teamwork required to produce a winner. Off-field clubhouse behavior is a bigger factor than you might suspect. I was in both good and bad clubhouse environments. I can tell you that a group of dedicated players, who get along, can generate a tremendous amount of pressure on a team of guys wandering on their own ego paths.

Winning teams have players who "give themselves up" to get a runner to third base with one out. Those are players who hit a ground ball intentionally to the right side of the infield just to get the runner to third and not care about their batting average. Good teams have infielders that will dive to stop a ball from going through the infield with a man on base no matter how badly the dive scrapes them up because (for the moment) it saves a run.

Winning teams are staffed by selfless individuals who glory in group success and are not swayed by individual press clippings or awards. When the owners find reason to pay one player 14 million dollars for one seven-month season, I hope you can see how things can go wrong if that player is self centered. It just spills onto the field and splits the unity needed to win. There is nothing like being rooted on by your peers who know they need your best effort to help the cause.

In my era there was no "big money." The game was played by guys who loved to compete and frankly, in most cases, knew little else.

All my good memories are of players who cared for and about each other and tried their very best to win.

Pitching: The Mental Game

Pitching a major league game in front of thousands is not as hard as one might think when it's what you have been trained to do from the beginning. What it takes though is a lot more mental concentration and awareness than you can imagine.

On days that I felt really good after warming up I had to be real careful about over-throwing. I found out early that there is nothing worse than feeling like you can blow a pitch by a good hitter if you haven't set him up for it. Good hitters can adjust to any speed and throwing a ball faster than normal has a tendency to straighten out the balls flight.

I might strike out the first guy and think, "OK! Now I'll breeze." It never worked that way. I was only good when I could retain pinpoint, narrowed down concentration of the strike zone set for the game by the plate umpire. When it's 110 degrees in Kansas City, it isn't easy. Or when the opposing lineup is loaded with long ball hitters, the effort needed to keep concentrating is wearing. Or when your shortstop throws a double play ball into the stands it doesn't help either. But you can never let it waver your resolve.

It's funny how sometimes you know you don't have your good stuff but it makes the game more fun. The hitters know it right away and they have a tendency to get more agitated with themselves if they don't fare well. It's at those times a pitcher starts to get the respect from the hitters because they see he is competitive and is willing to lay it all on the line without asking out of the situation no matter what the result. I can honestly say to you that I NEVER thought about quitting or worried about numbers. It was a matter of the manager giving me the ball to start the game and it was up to him to take me out when he couldn't stand what I was doing anymore. I never refused a start or asked out of one.

I remember a time in Fenway when I had pitched 9 innings and won and asked Higgins two days later if he wanted me to be ready if he needed an inning. He was adamant about the fact that he wanted me with 4 days rest and wouldn't use me on a bet. I'm sitting in the dugout without a damn thing on under my uniform when, I forget who, hurts his forearm late in the game and all of a sudden Higgins is looking down the bench at me despite a bullpen full of people. He gives me this silly grin and I kid you not, I go out there with no jock and no cup and a glove I borrow. I have never felt more naked and vulnerable in my life, but silly pride put me out there and I was lucky to survive the inning as they hit line shots right at my teammates. Naturally, Higgins never said a word to me about it ever. But that was the way it was in those days. If they said pitch, you pitched because you knew there was always some guy waiting to take your place.

CHARLES B. CAREY, BOSTON GLOBE

Top: The 1955 Red Sox pitching staff at Fenway.
Bottom: Me with my battery mate Sammy White.

One year I had to have a cortisone shot in my elbow every time I went out on the mound. That year everybody thought I was out of shape because I took so long between pitches. I was just trying to let the screaming pain calm down if a fastball was called for.

At the Major League level, I'd have to say that 90% of the game is played by using the mind. It's truly a wonder what a guy can do if he is willing to blank out pain and try to get better between the ears.

Place Your Bets

From the time I entered professional sports there was a "Golden Rule" drilled into my mind by the Red Sox that went like this: "Never wager on the game you are playing," period. It was also explained to every player I knew at that time that if they did they would be kicked out of the sport on their ear forever. There was no second chance offered and no probationary period. It was a one time deal very much like death! So when I tell you that I never bet on any game I played, I mean it, and you can bet the farm on that. You can also bet your mortgage that Pete Rose had the same instructions.

But all around us, as we played our games, the gamblers were like a shadow. In Fenway Park they had a spot out in right field. They used hand signals and had some way of recording the bets on each and every pitch thrown. The money was exchanged outside of the ballpark.

Then, on road trips when I was the starting pitcher, I would get calls in my hotel room from someone asking me who would be pitching tomorrow and say he was from some newspaper or wire service in some distant city. We were instructed to immediately hang up and report the call to our manager. Well, when you are a rookie, you'll find it doesn't do your cause any good to wake up your manager after he finally got to sleep after a bad loss or great victory for that matter, to report this everyday kind of thing. So, in the end, I just hung up on the caller but I always told my roommate or Tom Dowd the traveling secretary for the Red Sox at that time.

Since we are talking about gambling, I want you to know I am in the lowest of the success groups. I am unable to cope with the loss or manage the gain. I am a $20 person. I can live with any loss below but never above that figure and should I be $20 to the good, I have already figured out what I can buy with that for my shop in the garage and it's time to leave.

Still on the subject, I can report that Pete Runnels, when he was with the Red Sox, had a yearly wager with Nellie Fox of the Chicago White Sox on who would hit the most home runs. I can also report that it was unlikely for either of those two great players to be listed in the daily paper as doing that sort of thing. Knowing about the wager, I always threw Nellie a cross seam fastball as close to the middle of the plate as I could when there was no one on base and, instead of his normal wrong field swing for a hit with his choked up bottle bat, he would try and impress Pete and launch a ball that Jackie Jensen would catch 10 feet short of the fence in right field. Pete and I got along well.

Pitching in Different Parks

Today's lesson is, "Why pitching a baseball in different ballparks isn't easy." So listen up! Here is what I remember.

One of the problems was the distance from home plate to the backstop. For instance, if your home park is Fenway Park the distance is minimal and, therefore, visually you seem to be right on top of home plate and despite the fact that there are extremely few foul balls caught there, I always felt it was an advantage. The old Briggs Stadium in Detroit was the same, if not even closer.

So when a guy pitching in a visually small baseball park went to a place like Yankee Stadium or, in the old days Baltimore's Municipal Stadium or Cleveland's Municipal Stadium, it seemed home plate was a mile away. In those parks the catcher and umpire looked to be out on a tiny island miles from anywhere making for the feeling that any bad pitch would result in a "passed ball" and an easy advance of the runners if men were on base.

The reason I bring this up is because I have always felt it is harder for a pitcher whose home park is confined, close to the stands and intimate, to take his act to the spacious places. Conversely, a guy used to pitching in those big parks feels wonderful when getting in the small ones.

Then there is the fact that all pitching mounds are different and made out of different kinds of soil. Some have a steep drop-off toward home plate and others seem almost flat. All are supposed to be the same elevation above home plate but they weren't then and I'll bet my mortgage they aren't now.

The rubber pad that is used to push off for the throw is also never the same. Some are worn off on the leading edge and some are new and squared off. Then there is the matter of the soil immediately in front of the rubber. On some mounds the soil is easily removed and a hole develops. This can be a problem especially if you and the opposing pitcher are pitching from the same spot on the rubber because he is screwing around with your area. I learned to hook the inside spike over the rubber edge with the two other forward spikes staying on top so as to try and make all the pitching rubbers feel the same. I stayed out of the hole that the other guy was developing.

Then there is the critical landing area for (in case of a right hander) the left foot. Of all the things that can screw up throwing strikes it's that small area. I hate to bring this up but a devious groundskeeper can alter an opposing pitcher's landing area (if it's not the same as his pitcher) just slightly enough to make strikes just that much harder to throw. It really is a fascinating game.

Can I Have Your Autograph?

I have always wondered why and when obtaining an autograph in public became a God-given right. Personally, I would not walk across the street to get Noah's signature on a piece of the Ark if he motioned for me to do so! However, I accept the fact there are those hobbyists out there who enjoy collecting signatures and some who simply do it as a way to turn a profit. So, I find it incredible that being 41 years removed from the game of baseball that I still get about 15 requests a month to sign my autograph on chewing gum baseball cards, file cards, 8"x 10" pictures, baseballs, etc. These requests are accompanied by self-addressed stamped envelopes or boxes and I am delighted and honored to sign them. I believe that is how all autographs should be handled. Think back; this has evolved in only 55 or so years. In 1950 a "public figure" could, in fact, go out to dinner or to a movie or any place they pleased without the constant hounding by people who now feel it's their right to intrude on the moment. It's rude dammit! It's downright rude!

From my point of view it all started downhill in New York in the middle '50s when it became hard to get on the bus at the curb in front of the Commodore Hotel because a group of somewhat less than innocent kids would literally block the way. It got to be a pushing and shoving affair. Then some of their less than innocent parents started showing up. Same ones every trip.

Father to little Johnny, "Hey, there's one. Go get his autograph." "Hey Dad I got it!" "Great son, what's his name?" "Sullivan." "Who the hell is that, where is Ted Williams?"

Then when we arrived at Yankee Stadium; Father to little Johnny, "Hey, I know him! He is a ball player. Go get his autograph." Johnny to ball player, "Hey mister, can I have your autograph?" "Sure kid, what do you want me to sign?" "I don't know." " Well, if you haven't got anything to sign I guess you're out of luck kid." "Hey Dad, he won't give me an autograph!" Father to son, "Don't worry boy, he's a bum anyway."

The last straw with me came when a kid about 13 years old came up to me and asked me to sign a piece of paper. I did and when he looked down at my name he said, "Sullivan! I don't want a Sullivan!" and with that he unloaded his ink pen on my white shirt.

I assume I may have offended some of you who have received this public right. If so, I will be happy to sign your baseball card, but I have to warn you that you will need to gather 500 of my signed cards to trade for one Pedro Ramos. That's if you remember him.

Top: Opposing pitchers on opening day in Washington D.C.; me and Pedro Ramos.
Bottom: That's my dad in the dugout just to the left of Jackie Jensen, Ted Williams and Frank Malzone as they posed for spring training pictures in Scottsdale, AZ.

Team Travel

Unfortunately, distance became a factor in the Major Leagues because teams had moved west. The modern age had arrived and I, for one, hated it. Not the fact that the distance was greater, but that it meant we no longer could go by train.

I believe it also changed the game forever because there would no longer be a group of guys sitting together in a compartment talking over the game that was just played and get it all ironed out.

Unlike trains that were set to depart some hours after a game, the planes were mostly chartered and were ready the minute the game was over and were not, for some unknown reason, to be kept waiting. There was never enough time to calm down and stop perspiring after a shower. It would be a rush in a hot crowded bus (remember, buses were not air-conditioned then) to a plane waiting on the ramp ready to go. Even sometimes with the outboard engines running.

Instead of a leisurely couple of "POPS" in the lounge car and a great steak dinner with plenty of room in the dining car, it would be small airplane meal in a small seat beside a large sweating male body. Naturally, as soon as the air-conditioning of the plane took over, it was now paramount not to get cold with all your pores still leaking. The ultimate result was a very uncomfortable trip in wet cold clothes. At any rate, in planes, travel would never be the same. I'm sure the stewardesses shared my desire that we travel in trains. One told me she thought we would be better off going by camel since collectively we smelled like a caravan.

Back then access to the cockpit while in the air was common. I sat in the jump seat behind the co-pilot one late afternoon as we landed at Logan Airport, Boston, in ground zero visibility. The pilot, a veteran of the Berlin Airlift, did not touch the throttles until we slammed onto the runway. It took 20 minutes to taxi to the gate.

In fact, it went a lot further than that. The pilots would let us sit in their seats and fly the plane once we were at cruising altitude. Tom Brewer and I were regulars in the cockpits and used to bet on who could fly the plane the longest before the co-pilot would have to take over because our altitude or flying attitude was too bad to put up with. Some times our teammates would be hollering because we were spilling the poker chips and they couldn't keep the cards on the table in the lounge in the back of the plane. Remember? DC-4, DC-6 and DC-7s all had lounges in the back. At any rate, flying with one wing down and crab-wise wasn't always agreeable to the troops in the back.

The biggest problem with flying in those days? The ball club saw fit to provide only one lousy beer per player and I could never find a non-drinker to sit with.

Sore the Next Day

For me, there was no finer moment in the world than walking into a dugout after pitching nine innings and winning at the Major League level.

Afterwards, chugging on a cold beer and sitting worn out, half naked in front of my locker, the feeling of satisfaction was total. It was truly sublime.

Then, as if that wasn't enough, there is nothing like being on the field the next day during batting practice. You can sense the pitchers on the other team watching you with different degrees of envy. They knew how I felt and depending how their seasons were going, oozed different amounts of jealousy. I know. I did the same.

The good hitters, to a man, couldn't believe I got them out, but would concede with a smile and maybe a finger (which I always assumed meant I was number one). The mediocre hitters would avoid my glance as if it was the plague and when I looked at them directly and smiled, they would have preferred root canal work. The opposing managers would acknowledge the effort with a nod. They knew, and I knew, and the feeling was supreme.

On the down side, in my case, was the incredible soreness of the entire right side of the body due to the breaking down of body tissue caused by throwing as hard as humanly possible. From just behind my right ear to the right side cheek of my butt, it signaled "Out of order." The arm was unusable on the day after pitching. No brushing of the teeth or other sanitary functions with the useless limb.

Today the players are blessed with schooled trainers and modern medicine. In the fifties we were blessed with voodoo practitioners and old sayings. Today a pitcher leaves the game and puts his arm in ice. We left and put the arm in the 110-degree whirlpool. Today they drink all the water they can. We were given (I am not kidding) two salt tablets an inning on a hot day and told no water because it would make us sluggish. It was hard to get the mouth open the next morning.

It normally would take three days for the soreness to go away. Jim Bunning (the present day senator from Kentucky and Hall of Fame pitcher) whom I pitched against many times when he was with Detroit was, I believe, affected the same way because one day we met on the field the day after we had pitched against each other and shook hands left handed.

Jim Murray

One late afternoon, I sat on the lanai (porch) of the old Kauai Surf Hotel's Golf Pro Shop up on the cliff above Kalapaki Bay with a gentleman who couldn't play golf anymore because of his deteriorating eyesight. He was very close to being blind. He knew I had played in the Major Leagues and had his wife bring him up before she went off to have her hair done.

The man was Jim Murray, the Pulitzer Prize winning sportswriter from the Los Angeles Times. Murray was not your average sports reporter to say the least. Not even close. He was a lover of the people who labored at sports and was, with unusual candor, their best critic. He, unlike Howard Cosell, told it like it was. Jim never put himself above the people he wrote about but could be very caustic. He wrote with the freedom of not owing anything to anyone.

We talked about how strange it is that certain opposing players have incredible domination over others individually. Ray Herbet, a right-handed pitcher, got Ted Williams out regularly for eight years while pitching for Detroit and Kansas City. Vic Wertz, while playing for Cleveland, absolutely hit everything I threw at him as if he knew what was coming.

We talked of how difficult it is to throw strikes that can't be hit and the people who did it best. Almost in unison we said "Warren Spahn," who went from a power pitcher to a control artist of exceptional accuracy. Spahn only won 363 games and, get this, had 382 complete games! I told him about watching Sam White (lured out of retirement by the Milwaukee Braves with the biggest contract of his baseball career because their catcher Del Crandall got hurt) catch Warren in a game in Milwaukee. Sam put his glove out and looked at me in the Philadelphia dugout while Warren hit the pocket of his glove with the pitch. I explained to Jim that Warren had asked Sam to give him a signal for hitting the pocket and another signal for hitting the web of his catcher's mitt.

We laughed about the common warning from the manager to the pitcher after a time out and a meeting on the mound. "Throw strikes, dammit, but don't give him anything to hit."

Which took us into the final moments of our meeting as his wife Linda came back to get him. It was tough watching him struggle to see the front steps as I walked with him out to the car. I said, "I'm sure sorry about your eye problem Jim." "Not to worry Frank," he replied. "I probably have seen too much." Then he roared with laughter when I said, "If that was the case your lips wouldn't work either because some guys think you said too much."

With my hero, Warren Spahn, before a Jimmy Fund game.

Vin Scully

I have to say it once and for all, if you don't like the way Vinny calls a baseball game you probably don't like Christmas, 4th of July fireworks or a really nice shop tool for your birthday.

Vin Scully is the sole voice of the Dodgers baseball team but surely you can be big enough to overlook that small "nick in his character." Hey! I wish he were broadcasting for my favorite team too. He doesn't but he has my ultimate respect.

Just like the old days, he doesn't work with some idiot telling you what you just saw or what he just described. He does it alone without an opinionated fool who makes the whole game seem to hinge on World War 5. Vin just sits in his booth and describes the game with clear truth and candor. He doesn't try to make you a fan. He doesn't try to make you feel like the game is more important than life. He just paints a word picture that is easy to visualize and takes me back to the days when radio was all there was. Vin was the best then. Vin is the best now.

In the islands we get the Dodgers games when they are at home around (4:00 PM) and I always put the game on because I can easily keep up with the game and do something like write this with him in the background. He just said, "The ball landed like a marble on a tile floor," describing a bad hop and bailing the infielder out of the responsibility. See! There he goes again, being the best friend of the people he describes.

I met him on the very first road trip I took with the Boston Red Sox. It was in Philadelphia in 1953. The Dodgers had just finished a series with the Phillies and we had just arrived for a series with the Athletics. Sam White and I were walking by some little open door eatery and Vin, who was already seated with another man inside, yelled at us to join them. At any rate, I really didn't know who he was but enjoyed his company immensely. As I recall, he never once let on what he did. Sam knew and when we parted I asked Sam who the hell that nice red headed guy was. Sam said he was one of the broadcasters for the Brooklyn Dodgers.

Let's face it baseball fans, from 1950 to the present, this guy has been the granite we built our baseball house on. He is better at it today than ever and if California falls into the ocean during the baseball season I know the first thing we will hear from that re-configured coastline is Vin, back on the airwaves with his red hair in place and his, "Hi everybody and welcome to Dodger Baseball. Despite a small setback in time and a big setback in geography, the Dodgers have managed to attract another late arriving crowd here to the temporary ballpark in the new port city of Reno, Nevada."

Mindreaders

Watching television these days, I can only hope that those of you who study and love the game of baseball are, like me, just sick and tired of being told what the pitcher and catcher are thinking on every pitch, as if the announcer knew?

Listen! I've lived with my bride for 37 years and haven't a clue what she is going to do or say in every situation. While playing the game, I pitched to and roomed with catcher Sammy White, and we only had one serious conversation in eight years! So when I hear these commentators like Tim McCarver and Joe Morgan thinking they can actually foretell and relate the thinking of the players, I wonder if they shouldn't be transferred to the military so our GIs will know exactly what the enemy is pondering.

I can remember standing on the mound in Fenway Park and thinking, "Damn, this is a nice day!" "What could be better? Here I am facing Mickey Mantle and he is smiling at me." (Little did I know that he, Bill Skrowron, Whitey Ford and Don Larsen had spotted my VW Beetle behind the Kenmore Hotel and had lifted it up on the sidewalk and deposited it behind a telephone pole next to a brick wall. After the game I found my car with a traffic ticket on it and had to call a tow truck to get it out of the situation.) But, at that moment in the game, my thoughts were really not on any intense situation because I was enjoying the moment.

Hey! Baseball is a game! It is not war! The guys playing the game are doing it because they love it. Despite the press reports and the grimness and finality put on every move by the media, the players are having (excuse this) a ball.

In professional sports losing is not tolerated long, but can you imagine what mental wrecks the players would be if they all couldn't handle a loss? Let us keep in perspective that when two teams play, one can't win. My friend, Jim Murray, put it this way, "Show me a man who likes to lose and I'll show you a man that is playing golf with his boss."

We aren't talking about the Romans here, where "thumbs down" in the coliseum wasn't a good sign if you were lying on your back with a sword at your throat. So, lighten up Tim! Give us a break Joe! We just want to watch the game as it flows without the intense scrutiny of every damn moment.

If someone doesn't know by now how the game is played, forget it! Let them turn the TV channel to horse racing. Everyone can understand a horse race and I haven't heard anyone yet telling us what the horses are thinking. On the other hand, Sam White seemed to know.

AFTER BASEBALL

First Job after Baseball

I was released by the Minnesota Twins in August of 1963. I was crushed. Trying to right my shattered emotions and not wanting to burden the people I knew would take me in free of charge, I called Henry Hinckley, owner and prime mover of the Hinckley Boat Works in Southwest Harbor, Maine and asked if he had something for me to do at his place and I would work for nothing. Henry said for me to come up and run his repair dock for the rest of the summer. I found a room in a loft of a wonderful Italian family's home close to the wharf. In a sense, one life was over and another was about to start. I was 33 years old and about to meet the real world without a profession. Something all "jocks" had to face sooner or later in those days, as there were no millions or hundreds of thousands of dollars.

I had met Henry one day in Fort Lauderdale, Florida in a boat yard up the New River (that's the name) that runs through that city. He was a wiry man well under six feet and could hardly walk because of a bad back at the time. Knowing about him and his boats from my reading during the baseball seasons, there was nothing to do but pick up "my hero" and literally carry him in my arms whenever he wanted to go aboard a boat or up some stairs etc. We became great friends.

Anyone who has ever dreamed of owning a first class sailboat has always looked longingly at a Hinckley boat. If not, they should, because the craftsmen who have been employed there for generations are as good as our country has to offer. The boats not only look great and sail fast, they are state-of-the-art and all the components work! If they say there is electrical refrigeration, (rare in the early '60s on small boats) there is and it works. Henry told me it took him more than six years to convince his craftsmen that fiberglass boats would be the future of the business and they could still do their fine trim and interior wood work.

My job was to go aboard boats that came to the dock for repairs and see what was needed, then go into the factory and find the worker with the expertise to do the job. It was simple and, therefore, I was perfect for the job. The craftsmen hated breaking away from what they were doing and tried to ignore me. That's what most "downeasterners" did very well in those days. For instance, I ate in the same restaurant, at the same table, at the same time, every day at lunch for nine weeks and never once did the same waitress acknowledge I had ever been there before. Hell, after being booed by thousands, being ignored by a few people was easy for me and I can't remember a more wonderful time.

It worked. I was out of the game but content. With a deep breath of fresh air, I was ready to get on with my new life... but where?

Opposite: My first boat in dry dock at Westerly, Rhode Island, where I bought it.

Why I Stayed

Why Kauai? Well, for starters, it is incredibly beautiful to the eye. It is part of the remotest place in the world (Hawaiian Islands) and has the best temperature range of any place on the planet, period.

Baseball life was over for me and a new life that would certainly involve work (most people don't allow that being a jock is work) was to start. Since I had very little idea of what the hell I was going to do and, most of all, no idea how successful I would be, it might as well be in a place I could be in great weather digging a ditch. So, I sold the two houses I owned in Fort Lauderdale, Florida and told my parents (who lived with me at the time) to buy something they would be happy with back in California (which they both longed for) and I would take $5,000 with me to the islands. If I ran out of money, expect me back to stay with them until I wandered again.

I arrived on Kauai alone and rented a car (no mean feat then) and proceeded to drive northward. The sky was absolutely crystal clear on that February morning in 1964. As I drove, I came upon Wailua Beach, which had parking on the ocean side of the road in those days. I stopped because I hadn't been body surfing since I was a kid in Southern California. I went into the clean warm waves with complete joy. Simply put, I couldn't believe something this wonderful could exist. Back in the car, I drove to the north shore all the way to the end of the road at Haena. That was the clincher! Nothing I had ever seen before rivaled it. Driving back to Lihue and my room at Palm Haven across from the old Kauai Inn on Rice Street, I knew I would be calling Marilyn (wife to be) and say, "I think I found the place."

Some may say I lured the girl to the islands, and some may say I begged, but the fact that she gave up a great job in San Francisco to join me is in the books.

Later, after moving 7 times in 7 years, we were told about a half-acre view lot located close to the town center of Lihue, perched high on a steep slope above the many acres of the Grove Farm Museum property in the valley below. Here, we would make our stand! Marilyn and I would bring our cocktails in our yellow Volkswagen Beetle and park on our property-to-be and let the feeling of the place surround us. All the feelings were positive and the beauty of the views from early morning to late evening were perfect. So we took the financial plunge with great determination and, as I write this, we just paid it off. The cost of the house and property was unbelievably high at that time, but somehow we managed the $380.00 a month payments and history will support the fact that I never had to make that trip back to California.

Getting Married

I was shaving and Marilyn was getting dressed when there was a knock on the door. It was Juliet Wichman and I knew the moment I heard her say to Marilyn, "You're not going to the church with that "Son-of-a-Bitch," that she knew I was there and wanted me to know it. "You are being driven to the church by me, my dear!" That's how our wedding day started.

Loving Juliet Wichman wasn't hard for me. She spoke her mind like few others, but if you were straight with her, she was more than steadfast with you. She allowed me to stay in the apartment over the garage of her Haena home in 1965 when I was still single. This was before the hippies arrived to clutter the area. When that part of the island was sparkling clean; when I could stand naked under the outdoor shower and wash away the world as I had known it after a swim in the freshwater pool; when I had my "sticky rice" cooking in the pot on the stove to build a base of whatever I thought up for dinner; when I used a mayonnaise jar as my cocktail glass with a careful vodka tonic mix so I could walk down on the beach at sunset and watch Jack Hashimoto throw his net. All this was after manually working my butt off all day and knowing that sleep would be sublime. It was more than special.

Back to the wedding day. It wasn't that the lady's announcement was out of line. The reason for my bride's frown was because the dog hair in Juliet's car was enough to make a dozen rugs. But go to the church with Juliet she did and we were married. But what Marilyn heard the preacher say and what I heard him say still causes friction in this happy home. I heard him order her to honor and OBEY! That's what I heard!

Our honeymoon abode was one of the cliff cottages on the steep cliff that overlooks Kalapaki Bay and the Kauai Surf Hotel site, but before we could get to it there was the cocktail reception and dinner to attend in the brand-new Golden Cape special dining room atop that hotel.

It all went well with many toasts, etc., but I started realizing Marilyn was still blushed to the max. I passed it off as her deep satisfaction in obtaining my lifelong service never thinking it was because she was getting the flu. The flu it was and I mean she had it in spades. We parted company with the wedding party and I got her somehow up the hill into the cottage and clinically put her to bed.

Luckily, I had liberated a couple of bottles of champagne from the party and had managed to get them up the hill, too. So, after I put my love in bed, I went out on the lanai, overlooking the site I was hard at work helping to create. I found being married with a real job very satisfying. I found I was committed to both. I found the champagne wasn't bad either.

Sully and White at your Service

In the winter of '64, Sam White and I were working on the north shore of Kauai in Haena for a Mr. Kimball who owned a piece of Jack Harter's helicopter company, the Halekulani Hotel in Waikiki and the Waiohai Hotel on Kauai.

We were building a heliport at the base of the cliff on the west side of the Limahuli Stream. Our base was Camp Naue, the YMCA camp on the beach in Haena. Ours was heavy duty manual labor. Sam would stand up from digging and say, "To think between us we used to make $65,000 a year." Don't let me mislead you about Sam. He loved hard work. Put a cigar in his mouth and he would never quit, unlike his cohort, who would rather surf the bowl at Hanalei with Nick Beck and then have a beer with Henry Tai Hook the unoffical Mayor of Hanalei.

One Sunday afternoon on a very stormy rainy day, Sam and I needed to go to the property to see what the rain was doing to our project and with our future brides, Marilyn and Nancy, we hopped in my old Jeep Willis 4x4 station wagon as we knew the two stream crossings would be running hard. After checking out the site, which was handling the rain pretty good, we went to the end of the road to Kee Beach where the Napali Coast begins to see the high surf and then we headed back.

The stream crossing at the dry cave by the beach park was now even higher than when we had been through there earlier and now, stuck in the middle of it, was a rental car that had slightly missed the pavement crossing on the upper side with the right front wheel. I eased by it on the low side and we could see two couples in it. After getting through the stream, I turned around to face it as I had a four ton winch on the front bumper. It was pouring rain, but I had my bathing suit on and a rain jacket, so I took the end of the cable with a hook on it and got the cable hooked onto the frame of the rental car by laying down in the cold water which was now almost up to the doors and reaching under the car. I went back to the Jeep and put the winch in gear and out it came sweet as pie. I waved at them, got back into the Jeep and turned it around to leave, when in the driving rain the driver came to our door and motioned for me to lower the window which I really didn't want to do as I had just toweled off. He was in suit and tie and ruining both in drenching rain. I lowered the window slightly and he said, "I want to pay you for this." I said I was glad to do it and for him to get the hell out of the rain. He said, "But at least let me buy you a beer." I replied, "Okay if you insist," and he handed me $2.00.

I looked back at Sam, who shook his head and said, "That guy must have had something to do with our baseball contracts."

The Bull and the Barbed Wire

Before Princeville at Hanalei became the destination resort of today it was a whole lot of other things. First of all, it was and is a spectacular overlook to that magnificent bay. It was a Russian fort, also an artillery practice range in the 1940s, and in 1964 it was a cattle ranch where cows were up to their shoulders in grass.

Jack Midkiff was the ranch manager then and certainly one of the great characters to grace that area. He was married to Bernice, a very strong woman of conviction, but I thought the only girl that could emotionally afford Jack and they easily carved a place for themselves down on the beach road by the bay in Hanalei.

Sam White and I were building a helicopter pad next to the Limahuli Stream in Haena and Sam wanted some Chinese bamboo about 4" thick to build the hand rails to a small bridge spanning a 2-foot-wide stream that was taking the water we imported (by digging a stream bed by hand) from the bigger stream and putting it back into the same stream down the line so as to follow the law in Hawaii that says you can take water but not dam the flow.

Sam looked at me and said, "Go get some bamboo!" I said, "I got your bamboo right here pal! Who made you king?" He said, "Look, take your surfboard and check out the waves, then get some bamboo and I will have dinner waiting when you get back to camp." I said, "You got it, King!"

So I went first to the extremely small ranch office located about where the Princeville Shopping Center is today and barged in on Midkiff whom I had never met. He looked at me for a long moment before saying he would allow me to take some bamboo but not from the clump I wanted just past the bridge over the Hanalei River on the left side. He said the clump in the next pasture down was a lot more healthy and for me to go over his fence there to get the best pieces.

Hey! Is this day going alright or what? I parked my Jeep with surfboard on top next to the ditch that runs parallel to the fence and took my time getting over the barbed wire while looking at a small herd of cows that naturally sidled up to something different in their lives. I started to cut bamboo when I got this funny feeling that something was looking at me and when I turned around something was! It was the bull and he was already charging! With precious little time to retreat, I went back over the barbed wire on the run snagging my pants which caused me to land awkwardly in the ditch filled with a foot of water.

Safe, but shook, I immediately went back up to the office intent on kicking some Midkiff butt only to find Jack sitting on the door steps and smiling. He said, "It's best never to trust a stranger but now that we are friends, we better have a beer."

Trying to Burn Trees

John Hanohano Pa was born in Kalalau Valley and his family moved out of that remote area of the Na Pali Coast in 1932. When I met him he lived in a house on the beach at Wainiha and it was there that they ground taro to make poi. He was a wonderful old man and his stories of the old days were spellbinding.

In 1964, Sam White and I started working in Haena building a helicopter pad under Makana peak next to the Limahuli Stream for Jack Harter. The peak is known locally as "Fire Cliff" because in olden days the Hawaiians threw lighted spears off the very top. We started by clearing a small area on the three-acre site. It was virtually jungle with vines as high as thirty feet in the trees. I know because I fell out of one of the trees, but grabbed onto the very vines I was hacking away at and simply swung down to the ground like Tarzan.

I owned a Jeep station wagon which had a 4-ton winch on the front bumper. The small scrub trees could be pulled out of the ground and my intent was to burn all the trees and vines, etc. We only took out enough trees to allow the landing of the helicopter, but we dug fish ponds and cleared away a lot of underbrush. All went well until I tried to burn it all. It would start and then quit burning. I tried everything. I drove all the way to Lihue and picked up a load of old tires and ten gallons of kerosene, but the wood just refused to burn. One other thing; after the first attempt to burn, a dog showed up on the paved road below the area and started howling every time I'd light the fires.

A couple of days later, John Hanohano Pa came driving by in his old sedan and stopped as soon as he saw the dog. He walked up on the property and asked, "How long has that dog been here?" I told him I really didn't know, but the damn thing starts howling every time I light the fires. John shook his head and left.

The dog was black, thin, short-haired, sharp-faced with big sharp pointed ears that stood straight up, with unbelievable penetrating eyes. When I would approach the dog, it wouldn't scare and bolt; it just held its ground and stared.

Two days later as Sam and I ate our sandwiches for lunch, the dog unexpectedly came up on the property and I gave him a bite of my sandwich. When John Hanohano Pa came by later, the dog was asleep under my jeep. John yelled from his car, "Try burning now."

I guess I don't have to tell you how the fires burned and we never saw that dog again.

A few days later, I saw John and asked him about the dog and he just grinned and replied, "You wouldn't believe me if I told you."

Tougher than Unions

Wishard Brown was owner of the San Rafael Independent Journal newspaper when he was told by the FBI to buy a handgun. They taught him how to defend himself because there was big trouble with the newspaper union he was dealing with. The man stood like a rock through it all even when the FBI insisted he install metal bars on his home windows after two murders were linked to the strike and a number of his subscribers lost their store windows to violence.

I bring this up hoping you will allow that he was a man of principle and willing to defend what he thought right. He also bought one of the original 24 cottages on the cliff overlooking Kalapaki Bay and the Kauai Surf Hotel and with that ownership came the use of the entire hotel facility. If "Wish" wanted something, we would try our best to make it happen because he loved golf and contributed freely to the golf budget's bottom line.

He and I became more than "visitor/professional" friends. He always included my bride and me at his parties and dinners, etc. Whenever he was "on island" there were the poker games, too.

I also need to report that Wishard had a tendency to let his hair down a bit upon arriving in the islands. No, let me re-phrase that. Wish came to Kauai to let it all hang out.

For instance, once he and his wife Shirley were seated across from each other in the Golden Cape Restaurant atop the Kauai Surf Hotel and, not only had they had a few "clears" before arriving, they were well into another batch when she said something that so incensed the man that he picked up his glass of water and threw it at her. (When Wish related the story to me later he said, "It's always important to have a glass of water at your table so you don't have to throw your drink!") At the very moment he tossed the water, Shirley moved her head to the right and down to find something in her purse. The water missed her and continued on over the back of their booth to the adjacent one and hit a lady sitting with her husband squarely in the face. Wishard got up immediately to render his apology and make the situation right, but Shirley, still unaware of the errant throw, thought Wishard was making a pass at the man's wife.

To this day, the help in that room says the situation in that wonderful restaurant went downhill faster than a cannon ball dropped off the Eiffel Tower.

When Wish related the event to me I asked him if his wife knew about his gun. That wise old bastard looked at me as if I was crazy and said, "You think unions are tough?"

Fly Casting can be Fun

There is an old Hawaiian proverb that goes like this:

> If you wish to be happy for one hour, get intoxicated.
>
> If you wish to be happy for three days, get married.
>
> If you wish to be happy for eight days, kill your pig and eat it.
>
> If you wish to be happy forever, learn to fish.

I concur with the above. Well, most of it. I had been happy with rod and reel until one day I decided to learn to fish with a fly rod. Casting needs some practice. Strike that. It needs hours of practice. Especially in the island winds and I gave it a lot of effort on our front lawn until the kid next door yelled over to me as he went up the steps to his house, "Even grass carp need water Mr. Sullivan."

That did it. I took all the gear to the small boat harbor at Nawiliwili. I walked along the levee that surrounds three sides of the boat dock area and spotted a barracuda motionless in the water. It was the perfect situation. All that the moment cried for was a lure gently placed about a foot in front of the fish. I picked up the tip of my rod quickly letting the line float back over my head perfectly but started forward with the rod too soon which took all the steam out of the cast and the lure dropped too low and caught up on a small bush behind me. I thought, "OK, you're new at it so just take your time." I retrieved my line and got the lure out of the bush and peeked over my shoulder to see if the fish was still there. It was!

The barracuda was being very patient with me and I was thinking, "It is being willed that I catch this fish, so get it all together and make one good cast." The result of this was that my next cast was too much overhand letting the right to left wind put the hook neatly under my right hip back pocket. Damn! Now the only way to extract the hook was to take off my pants which was something I really didn't want to do standing out on the levee like a monument. It meant lowering my pants below my knees to be able to twist the garment around enough to get access to the hook. Here I glanced over to see if my fish was still there causing me to lose my balance and having to sit down quickly to avert a tumble down the rocks. This motion served to put the hook deeper in the material and now I literally had to cut the hook out leaving a hole in my pants.

Across from me on the boat dock was a young couple working on their sailboat and now they had put their tools down and were watching. I struggled to my feet and when the next cast took my hat off I heard their laughter. I picked up a rock and threw it at the fish and both he and I left the area. He with his dignity.

Now I make sure the kid next door is in school.

Top left: With son Mike out in front of the Hyatt Hotel on Kauai.
Top right: I'm trying to lift the halibut I caught on light tackle in Alaska.
Bottom: Belly boating at one of the many hidden places on Kauai."

Darrell and I

At last count (mine) there are 64 reservoirs on this magnificent island of Kauai. Almost all were built to supply sugarcane with the required amount of irrigated water needed for a healthy crop. (One ton of water for one pound of sugar.)

Once introduced to these bodies of water and the ditches that fed them, the big mouth bass flourished because the run off of chemicals from the cane fields created algae in the lakes and the smallest of fish had something to chew on.

At any rate, the result of the above has made for the finest bass fishing anywhere I have ever been. Yes, Jack Wilhelm and I carried my 12 ft. aluminum boat over fences and slid the boat down the sloping sides of the many man-made water catches in some of the remotest places you can imagine. We fished so many times without seeing a soul it was like a two-week vacation in 4 hours. Yes, we bought an electric motor and carried the batteries with us which made lugging enough beer even more stressful. It was always a contest and we had names for every pond. For instance, one cloudless brilliant morning in "Bandman's Pond" Jack beat me 24 to 21. Not bad for 3 hours of fishing. Of course Jack used the Carolina rigged worm that I refuse to call fishing! By the way, we always catch-and-release every fish in fresh water.

All of this was fun and agreeable to me because I could hold my own with Jack, but then he brought along his son-in-law, Darrell. How was I to know this young guy was a more than gifted caster of any type of fishing rig known to man? How was I to know I would never even hold a candle to his aggressive success? Despite my fishing with Darrell almost every Saturday for 2 years, I can't remember a time he didn't catch more fish or a time when I had more fun losing.

Let me stop here and tell you about bass fishing. The best lure caster wins! Bass are lazy but if you can drop a lure within a few inches of one the strike is inevitable. The result was, Darrell wins!

To explain how deep we were into fishing every weekend no matter what the weather, Darrell and I almost died one late morning while driving back into Lihue after fishing hard for 5 hours. We were doing 50 miles an hour across Halfway Bridge with Darrell driving his truck pulling my boat. I was thumbing through a bass fishing catalog and asked Darrell to take a look at the lure I was endorsing. He took a peak, but did look up in time to miss by an inch a car stopping to make a rare left turn into the quarry. I still don't know how the boat stayed on the trailer but because of Darrell's quick reaction the swerve saved our lives.

It's always good to be with the best.

The Juice

I have a confession to make. I was a big O.J. Simpson fan. For starters, I went a couple of semesters to the University of Southern California and somehow was instilled with Trojan pride despite not playing sports for the school or graduating. Maybe it was my relationship with the Kappa Sigma fraternity. Other than going through their "HELL WEEK" alone, I can't remember a part of my life that was more fun. They put me through "HELL WEEK" during the Christmas holiday break because I had to go to spring training and the fraternity house was pretty empty except for the guys who couldn't afford the trip out of state to their homes. They weren't exactly a happy bunch of campers and seemed to relish in my struggle.

First I was given a toothbrush and bar of soap and made to scrub the eating hall's floor. The hall easily handled 40 - 50 people. I was on my hands and knees for more than two days. I was given a traditional gunny sack to wear with nothing under which would have been okay except for two ugly factors. 1) With my height it barely covered my shortcomings. 2) Since the fraternity had closed the kitchen, I had to walk four blocks to a diner and eat in public wearing only you know what. What made it really ugly was the dead lobster I had to have with me for a week. In the end the people at the diner would just hand the burger out of the back door not caring if they got paid or not.

When O.J. came to the Hula Bowl in Honolulu I was stoked and told my wife I was leaving her to see the Juice. Bob Herkes (VP of Inter-Island Resorts at the time) held a terrific bash at his house for all of us from the out-islands and provided the ride to the stadium with his Hilo Sampan bus.

The problem was weather. It had been raining for days. The field in the old stadium didn't have a tarp and should have only been used for mud wrestling, but to hell with it I was committed and willing. Smugly, I had my big golf umbrella and could care less about the rain because I would finally see my man in person.

In less than a dozen plays you could not tell who was playing who and finally they gave the ball to my hero and he took it 90 yards to score. Only reason I knew it was him was his unique style. Meanwhile, there was another problem. This guy behind me kept complaining about my umbrella blocking his view. He tapped me on the shoulder and related his concern and I finally relented to his wish just so I wouldn't cause a scene in front of my bosses. I folded the umbrella and got soaked.

Just before the half was over an usher came up with a guy behind him and told the bastard behind me to get the hell out because he didn't have a ticket! I should have sensed right there that being an O.J. fan was bound to end badly.

Palmer Comes to the Kauai Surf

Arnold Palmer is coming to the Kauai Surf Hotel to do a United Airline commercial? What? You mean Arnold Palmer? The real Arnold Palmer? But we only have 9 holes! Can this be true? It was true in 1968 and, believe me, the man was wonderful to one and all.

I don't know how he is now, but let me tell you that Arnold Palmer was a clean piece of paper then, a dynamic man that let you into his world. He treated every person he met like they were someone who was his pleasure to know. He made sure the cart boy and the shoe polisher were taken care of and he would put that grin on them while telling them to make what they did special.

This reporter was an assistant golf pro working under Bill Schwallie at the time and Bill allowed me to do everything with him when it came to Palmer's visit.

After the first day of filming, Arnold asked Bill and me to lunch with him down by the pool at the coffee shop. There, he admitted to us that his aluminum shafts were suspect and that he had played a round of golf some months prior with old hickory shafts against an alternate shot with the aluminum ones and, in his own words, said "there wasn't a whole lot of difference."

The man loved hitting golf balls like no other I had ever been in contact with. He stood on the second hole of that old layout and must have hit 30 balls trying to reach the green some 330 yards away. Then glancing to his right he spotted the first red channel marker buoy marking the entrance to Nawiliwili Harbor and fired another 30-40 balls out into the water trying to hit it. Schwallie elbowed me and whispered, " I hope I ordered enough golf balls for him."

Arnold put on a golf clinic for us and I thought he'd never end it. Everyone who was housed in the hotel at the time went away knowing this man was a special person. Personally, I must tell you that few people that high on the celebrity chart could match his act in those days and we had a host of top names visit us over the 27 years I spent on that property under the different hotel names.

Later that year we were told they needed to re-film some fly-over scenes and for us to get a stand-in for Palmer who could not be there. Mike Calhoun was elected to be the stand in for Arnold because he was the same height and weight. It's a good thing it wasn't a close-up. Now, Calhoun is no narrow shouldered guy. In fact, he is a damn good example of a guy ready for anything and willing to back it up physically, but Palmer's shirt made Mike look like he was at a pajama party.

Thankfully, they never filmed Mike's swing with a golf club. I can only say that it resembles a used truck tire swinging from a rope off an ugly tree.

The King and I.

What Was Left of the Invasion

Six hundred miles east of Mindanao (Philippines) and seven degrees above the equator lies the island nation of Palau. Truly one of the wonders of the world. It is a limestone monument to time and a undersea mind-blower!

Peleliu is the southernmost island within the Palau barrier reef. During WWII, because General MacArthur didn't believe in aircraft carriers and there was an airstrip being used by the Japanese on that island, the inevitable took place. It was so bad that the U.S.Army had to relieve the U.S. Marines to finally secure the place after months of brutal fighting. No, I can't pass it off as brutal. It was slaughter on both sides, as American and Japanese commanders kept sacrificing men to gain a piece of jagged coral hell that in the end turned out useless.

In 1976 Les Eichhorn and his wife, Lou, and the Sullivans were there housed in the Continental Hotel on the island of Koror. Les was a friend of the manager of Van Camp's fisheries who was, for the moment, back in the USA. Luckily he had directed his assistant manager, Marcello Pierantozzi to take care of us. Little did we know he would take those orders to mean treat us like we were royalty. He invited us to visit the home of his wife's grandmother who was the High Priestess of Peleliu. Six of us got in a 16 ft outboard and traveled the 45 miles of flat water inside the Palau barrier reef. We sped by one small island after another skimming the clearest water in the world. It was as if we were flying over the bottom.

Being guests of the Priestess, we toured the island in the back of the only pickup truck driven by Sandra's (Marcello's wife) uncle, Ah Sam. As a combat veteran, I was appalled with what was still left on the island just waiting to be set off. I was also emotionally blasted by the frightful coral terrain men lost their lives over. It was jagged and sharp and if you fell you would be badly cut. To think men being shot at had to crawl on it had me shaken.

At one point I got in a ruined tank and bore-sighted its cannon then jumped out and ran across a dirt road through shoulder high grass to find a mouth of a cave with the very gun used to destroy the tank still aiming at it. It got to be like a bad dream as it took me back to man's ultimate failure, WAR! We walked down into an underground Japanese officer's bath house. The walls were made of no less than 6' thick concrete with 2" thick re-bar. Unbelievably there was a clean hole through the wall from one of our battleship shells that was a dud.

Finally, I climbed to the top of Bloody Nose Ridge and there was a small monument that read, "Lest we forget the thousands of men who died here." I sat there alone for a moment grieving, knowing the world already has.

Meeting Carey with Dallas Green

The year was 1985 and who should arrive on Kauai via a cruise ship with a horde of Chicago Cubs fans but my former Phillies teammate, Dallas Green, and his wife Sylvia. I'm not sure what position he held in the Cubs organization then. He was either the manager or the general manager of that organization. What did I know? I was no longer in the game. It really didn't matter to either of us.

Dallas is a wonderful, loud, gregarious human being whom I have admired from the time we were struggling right-handers with a Phillies team that made every pitcher struggle. Sylvia is a smart, good-looking, independent girl who Dallas can't fool and when she smiles it makes everyone around her feel better.

Marilyn and I were invited on their helicopter tour and afterward we all went to a Mexican place on Rice Street in Lihue for lunch. Some loud guy came into the place and before I could say something about the man, Dallas stood up and introduced me to him. It was Harry Carey, the long time play by play broadcaster of the Chicago Cubs. Harry was in great voice and, between Dallas and Harry, it was like eating with the radio turned up loud on a comedy station.

I met Dallas under the worst of circumstances. I had been traded to the Phillies because their manager Gene Mauch wanted me there. Why? He said he wanted me to help settle down the Daulton Gang. Hello! I knew nothing about the National League other than pitching against them in spring training and in an All-Star Game and the only Daulton Gang I ever heard of was in the old wild west. Mauch had me room with Turk Ferrell, whom I found was a great guy despite his carrying a hand gun in his suitcase. We got along great. This very good relief pitcher, despite the handicap of a polio left leg, was a tall, brash at times, willing-to-go-along-with-anything type of guy except when flying in airplanes. He once said to me, as we took off from a snowy Denver runway, "Look at my hands." He held them palm up as the plane took off and all of a sudden there was enough water in his palms that he could dump them! I sat there shocked at what I had just seen. It kind of mirrored the troubling times I had with that club and the "darling of the press," Gene Mauch. I agree he knew a lot about baseball, but baseball is played by guys who need to have their manager's support.

My time in Philadelphia isn't a good memory nor was what I did on the mound, but getting to know Dallas Green and his bride was worth it all and a few years later when the Phillies named him the manager, I knew there would be greatness, because I was confident that he would never make the same mistakes with the troops that Mauch had.

Canoe Club Coach Achi

There is a wrong assumption out there that athletes are born to the task and merely take the next step to stardom. I will argue that most, at least in my day, were dragged out of school hallways by win-hungry coaches. Today, I think the parents are the driving force, but forever there have been those challenged verbally by people already committed to the chore. These committed people have a tendency to suggest that to deny their request would leave you without, in the case of males, testicles.

The latter was the case when I was stopped in front of the Post Office in Lihue, Kauai by Duke Wellington and verbally prodded to join the Kauai Canoe Club in 1964 to aid in their quest to win the Hawaii state title. Little did I know there was a Stanford Achi (coach) in the formula or that paddling a 6-man outrigger racing canoe is the hardest work a man can do sitting down.

It could be said of Stanford Achi that he was less than kind to a mainland "haole" and was frequently found screaming racial insults at him. Practice was every day but Sunday and never lasted less than 3 hours, which means you might rest your paddle a total of 10 minutes in that time. Yes, there are blisters on the butt. Yes, you will be paddling a canoe in practice with an old tire on the bow to impede movement through shallow water that in itself resists forward progress. Simply put, it is hell.

But, if nothing else, once committed to a challenge, I show up and I compete with the stubbornness of a mule to see who wins or loses. And so it went until we got to Hilo Bay on the Big Island and the state meet.

Duke and his crew won their junior race easily in record time and, amazingly, all the rest of us followed with impressive stuff and, when it came to the last race, Kauai was leading in the standings. Unfortunately, we had no senior crew for the last race which was needed to clinch the meet.

Suddenly Stanford was looking at me saying, "I need a crew; will you be #4?" "Only if you'll go," I said, knowing he wasn't in shape to do the 2 mile race. He just looked at me and stepped into the canoe in the #3 seat in front of me.

We didn't win the race, but gave it a hell of an effort and during it I had a lot of satisfaction talking to Stanford about how his relatives would be ashamed of his puny effort. As I spoke, just loud enough for him to hear, I could see the back of his neck getting redder. When the race was over, as we got out of the beached canoe, Stanford turned quickly toward me and I thought the fight would be on, but he smiled and put his hand out; it was a natural, we became great friends.

Top: My great friend Stanford Achi and I at a shopping center outrigger canoe display.
Bottom: The Friday afternoon scramble mob.

Sam Flies His Glider

Among many other things, Sam White enjoyed building remote control models. And while working at Princeville on Kauai, he entertained himself with a boat model of a Chris-Craft runabout. It was about two and a half feet long and was powered by an electric motor. It went nicely around the lake at the 9th hole of the Lakes Nine on the Makai Golf Course. People playing well seemed to enjoy it, while those folks not hitting the ball as good, would just as soon he took his little boat and shove..... oops! Not only am I straying from the story, but those folks would not have to wait long before the boat came to an ugly end anyway. One day Sam decided to trail a short line with a fishing lure off the back of his boat. The boat was last seen being pulled under by an eight-pound big mouth bass.

But the time I remember the most was at the Kauai Surf Golf Course. It was a Friday and all the regulars were assembling for the weekly 12:00 "scramble" golf match. Sam walked into the pro shop and under his arm was a glider wing at least six feet long. He was all excited and said, "I'll go get the rest of the model and let's fly it." I had to tell him we would lose our start time if we didn't tee off right away and it would be better if he flew it later when we finished.

Our scramble matches always ended up in the bar next to the pro shop and eleven of us were having a few "pops" while Sam was busy anchoring a long rubber launching line in the middle of the fairway about even with the 75-foot lone palm tree that signaled the left turn to the first hole. We ordered another round of drinks and watched as he stretched the line almost back to the first tee. Then he asked one of the cart boys to hold the glider until he signaled to let go. He then ran down the fairway next to the tree and picked up the remote control panel.

This was our signal. We grabbed our drinks, piled into carts, headed down the fairway and parked a little distance from Sam. He proudly looked over at us and called to the cart boy to release the glider. The long rubber band recoiled perfectly and the glider swooped up gracefully into the air. The rubber line came loose at the right moment but the glider took a slight left turn and crashed directly into that lone palm tree.

There was an awful silence broken only by the sound of glider pieces falling to the ground all around Sam. He stood there wide-eyed and looked over at me. I hollered at him, "Forgot to turn the remote control panel on, yeah?" He could only nod his head "yes" as we drove by booing him on our way back to the bar.

Later, when he came into the bar, we stood as one to give him a standing ovation and toasted him for a great afternoon!

A Cart in the Lake

A Mr. Pott walked into my office at the Kauai Surf Hotel golf pro shop and announced to me that he had a problem. I sat back in my chair, thankful for the break from the tedious daily reports, and said, "Well, I'm sure we can fix it." I had pretty much seen it all over the years and knew that helping a person is very beneficial to the business as the good will created is priceless. On the other hand, if it was a complaint, he still had come to the right guy. After all, I was the "leader of the band" and could refund his money or give him future rounds of golf or anything needed to appease and rectify the situation. "What's the problem?" I said. "My clubs are in the lake to the left of the fourteenth tee," he answered. It didn't surprise me. I had retrieved clubs from trees, lakes, oceans, roof tops and fish ponds etc. I said laughingly, "What did you do, throw them in?" "No," he replied. "They are on your cart." Light Bulb!!!! .... Whoa! Now we both had a problem.

Electric golf carts, if pulled out of fresh water fast enough, only suffer a couple of solenoid failures as long as the motor is not running. In salt water just forget it. So, I was now in a rush to get the chain we had for that very problem and get out to the pond. Mr. Pott stopped me and said, "You don't understand. I am in a golf match and need another cart and one of your rent sets." That was a new twist for me. "Er, ah, I see." I stammered. "You need to get out to your match." "Yes, I'm leading one up!" So I had the counter people fix him up as I took one of the cart boys with me out to the pond. On the way I called maintenance and told them to meet me with a tractor at the 14th tee. All the cart boys who worked for me were instructed to keep a bathing suit in their locker just for this event, and the boy dove and attached the hook on the end of the chain to the back of the cart. We had the cart out of water in minutes. In the cart was Mr. Pott's wallet with his gold watch wrapped around it, his money clip fully loaded with more than just a couple of bucks, a pair of Florshiem shoes, a beautiful alpaca beige sweater and his car keys.

He had rejoined his two friends and had finished the 14th hole and was just now coming up on the other side of the pond playing the 15th. I waved at him and yelled that we had his stuff. He gave me a disinterested look, a half nod, and hollered, "I'll get them after the match."

The cart boy said, "Man, they must have some kind of big money game going for him not to even want to see if all his stuff is here." I told him I'd try and find out. I'm sorry I did. When he came in to settle up, I asked him about the match. He was really excited about winning $4.00 from each of the two men. The solenoids cost him $32.00 each.

Turtle Tears

Roger Bird was the manager of the Golden Cape Restaurant in 1969. This was the newest and best eatery on the island and was situated on top of the Kauai Surf Hotel with a marvelous view of Kalapaki Bay and the surrounding mountains. While dining there, if you looked out to your left, there was a small white lighthouse on the point overlooking the entrance to Nawiliwili Harbor.

It was there, while fishing one morning, that Roger hooked something big and knew right away, if he ever got it bested, he would need help pulling it up the steep rock face surrounding the point. Roger's girlfriend, Nancy, was sunning herself above him and he yelled to her to go and find help. Nancy ran back past the 23 cottages perched on the cliff above the bay to the first one which housed our Golf Pro Shop. Bill Schwallie and I responded to her plea by jumping in a golf cart and racing down the first fairway past the second tee to where we could see Roger still battling something big. We then scampered down the steep slope and onto the lava outcropping in our street shoes and helped Roger bring up, of all things, a Green Sea Turtle (Species = chelonia mydas). What a prize!

Those were the days when the turtles were not protected and if you ever had Green Turtle steak you would not forget the finer than veal taste. The turtle had a shell of at least 24 inches across and was hooked by its right front flipper. We got the hook out and I said to Roger that I'd go home and get my knife and have it cleaned in no time. That was before the turtle looked up at me with its big wide child-like eyes and, because being out of water affected them, began to have tears roll down either side of its beak.

Quickly I said to Roger, "If I was off work I would, but I still have some hours to go." Roger said, "I'll just take it down to the chefs in the main kitchen."

Before leaving the property that afternoon I called the main kitchen and asked the chef if they had cleaned the turtle. He hesitated and said, "The damn thing is crying like a baby down here and none of the daytime guys want to do it. So I'm leaving it for the night shift." The next day when I got ahold of Roger on the phone, he told me the rest of the story.

The nighttime chefs were no better killers and they finally released it into the koi pond by the Outrigger Dining Room. The turtle quickly devoured four of the prized carp and was taken out of the pond and released the next morning back into the ocean in front of the hotel to the applause of a few guests.

I guarantee you, those guests had never tasted what they were applauding or they might be mourning the moment.

Lovejoy Launches a Shearwater

Glenn Lovejoy was the general manager of the Kauai Surf Hotel. He made the hotel what it was, which was simply an island jewel. Those of us working there, worked for him and not necessarily Inter-Island Resorts, the owners. Glenn was innovative, gregarious, tireless and totally accessible.

Shearwaters are sea birds with a wing span of about two and a half feet. They spend most of their life out at sea feeding off small bait fish or the residue of larger fish attacks on smaller fish schools. Fishing boats try to spot these birds circling over the action for their own success. They nest in windy cliffs, close to the water and when their young are ready, they are kicked out of the nest by the parents who are tired of feeding them. Civilization then becomes a problem as the lights at night shining off a wet surface makes it look like water to them. So they may land on a highway or a roof top, etc.

One slammed into Glenn's office on a rainy night via the open lobby. When he found it in the morning, it seemed fine and was pecking his hand as he brought it into the lobby. Naturally, people were fascinated as he moved toward the elevators. Glenn gladly explained to them that it was standard procedure on Kauai to gather these fledglings and put them back into the wild. He then invited them to watch him launch the bird into the air and see it fly off to its own environment, the sea. It took both elevators to transport the group to the top.

The scene was set. Lovejoy announced he was ready and the people were poised at the railing of the ten-story building. Satisfied that all the people could see and, with an all-knowing look on his face, he tossed the bird skyward with both hands. The launch was perfect. The bird was head up and steady as it reached the apex of the arc and now as it slowly nosed over, it was time for the bird to spread its wings and take flight. Sadly, I must report, the shearwater did nothing. The bird made nary a peep or a wing flap. It simply plummeted downward. If you had been there, you would have heard Lovejoy say, "fly... come on fly... FLY... for Christ sakes... FLY!" Well, I am even sadder to report that the bird hit the concrete below so hard it didn't even bounce. There was total silence on top of the hotel building. Lovejoy moved away from the railing to face the incredulous stares of the once friendly group. There were whispers of "murderer, should be reported; I won't stay in a hotel run by this killer, etc." Then, while he was trying to explain that it had never happened before, they separated themselves from him. He was left to ride the elevator down alone.

Hey! Glenn! Even NASA doesn't have a perfect launch record.

Sam and I Get Locked Out

The last time I roomed with Sam White was 1978. It was at the Kuilima Hotel on the north shore of Oahu. We were both there to take a very difficult test for entry into the PGA of America. The pressure was enormous as both of us were already managing golf operations for large corporations. Sam was running the Princeville operation for an oil company out of Colorado and I was doing the same for Inter-Island Resorts and failing these tests would be a grim sign to our bosses, who needed the PGA to sanction tournaments on their properties. The classes and test were over a four-day period. The test was rumored to be a bitch!

On the last day, after the "true to the rumor" test was over, we played a round of golf on the hotel course with two of the other guys and finished about six o'clock and then found a bar off the main lobby. I was totally exhausted and, after a few "snaps," said to Sam, "I don't give a damn what you are going to do, I am going up to the room, shower, call room service and hit the hay!" For once, even Sam was beat and said, "I'm coming with you." I would later regret it.

In the room we called for a few more drinks and took our time. I showered first and put on a pair of jockey underwear. We ordered dinner and Sam showered and just wrapped a towel around his waist. There was only one chair in the room so when dinner arrived on a big tray we took the phone off the night stand and put it between the beds and put the tray on it.

I remember it as a damn fine meal and when it was over I said to Sam, "Put the drink glasses on it and I'll carry the tray out into the hall so we don't step on it in the middle of the night." He said, "Good, I'll get the door for you." The tray was now overloaded and as I bent over to put it on the floor in the hall, a couple of bottles started to fall off and Sam took a step out the door to catch the bottles. CLICK! You guessed it. It was the door! You're right. No Key! What else? The elevator door was opening! Yeah, a crowd of people were coming our way. That's right, jockey shorts and towel, that's all.

As the group came down the hall, I tried to sink deeper into the alcove to the door of our room but just as they got even with us, Sam pointed his finger at me and said in a clear voice, "He is the pervert!"

A couple broke away from the group and, without saying anything, went into the room next to ours. I quickly went to the door and knocked. I could plainly hear the wife say, "Don't open that door Harry!" So I hollered through the door for Harry to call the bell desk and have someone bring us a key. Then, with great resolve, I said to Sam, "Separate rooms from now on White!"

The Golf Ball Deal

I have always been of the school that a handshake seals a deal and only a weasel would back out of it. That said, I think it was in 1979 a young man walked into my office at the Kauai Surf Golf Course and said, "I'll dive in the lakes and collect all the errant golf balls if you will pay me 9 cents a ball for the ones you want back." Thinking about it for the first time I replied, "Why would I want to do that since I could dive in the lakes and get them for nothing!" Then he said, "OK, why don't you do that then?" "Because," I said, "I don't want to stick my head in that ugly muddy water!" At that, he smiled like a Cheshire cat and said, "That's why we should talk further about me diving in your lakes and getting all the balls." Then I thought, "I could get a koa bowl to put a pile of used golf balls in and sell each ball for 50 cents!" So it was agreed that the next day he would start diving in the lake near the 16th hole and we shook hands. Before he left he asked me how many of the balls I would like. I said, "All of them!" Thinking, "hell, there can't be that many."

The following day, after remembering the previous day's deal, I jumped into a golf cart to see if the guy had showed up at the lake. What I saw at the lake edge shocked me. Stacked along the shore were eleven gunny sacks full of ugly dirty golf balls and he was still underwater getting more. All in all he pulled up 27,682 balls in the three lakes on property. Holy Jesus! Where in hell was I going to get the $2,491.38 to pay the guy off.

Late that afternoon he came in and I was searching for an out by telling him I didn't want the dirty ones. He just kept smiling and said, "I know that and you don't want the cut ones either, right?"

That evening I pondered the situation and wondered how I was going to pay the guy or "weasel out of the deal." I was consoling myself that it would take him a hell of a long time to clean all those balls and I would have a few days to come up with an idea when the phone rang. It was a friend who said, "Hey, Sully! You missing any golf balls?" "No, why?" He then proceeded to tell me, "I got a call from the restaurant across the street from my laundromat complaining about a roar coming out of the place bothering the people eating." I said, "You don't mean someone is washing and drying 27,682 golf balls do you?" "That's what I'm about to tell you pal. Not only that, the balls came out looking brand new!"

To this day, I always think a deal all the way through before I promise anything because I had to sit down with the ingenious Dan Matheny and beg him to let me pay him in installments.

Remembering Willard

We leave the dock at 6:30 AM on this Sunday, December 10, 2000, which is the same time we have been leaving it for 20 years in one boat or another. As usual, I am busy helping out with the different chores required for departure. I will also select some of the fishing lures that will be set to start the day's fishing. They have to be connected to each of the eight poles surrounding the aft cockpit where all the action will be aboard Maleka Nui, the 54' Bertram boat, owned by Rick Ellis.

As we leave the harbor still in the dark, I can feel the heave of the boat and here on Kauai, the moment you leave the harbor you can get a real read on what the day will be like. Today it is an easy swell moving in from the east and light winds. When we push out past the headlands, it is obvious we are going to be treated to an incredible sunrise. In fact, ninety miles away, the Island of Oahu is framed by the tip of this morning's rising red ball. It's awesome! A sight to stir the soul.

I can't help reflecting on this sun that is rising so beautifully for me, has just set on the life of my friend and teammate, Willard Nixon. I go down to the back deck and sit on one of the fish boxes alone and I don't deny crying. Here I am watching one of the most glorious sunrises while alive and healthy and Willard's luck has just run out.

Willard was a pitcher with the Red Sox from 1950 to 1958 and, among his many wins, were 51 complete games. I'll bet half must have come against the hated Yankees. I know, being a native Georgian, hating the Yankees is a birthright but he beat them like a drum. Willard lost his memory late in life, but my memory is vivid and I want his kids to know my memory of Willard will always be of him standing tall on the mound in Yankee Stadium with the 95-plus degree heat bearing down, and despite 45,000 fans screaming against him, he would be resolute and dominating and the likes of Mantle, Berra, Skowron and Bauer would have to take the long slow walk back to their dugout after failing against him.

Willard worked in the off-season as a chemist in a textile mill to make ends meet. Like most ball players of his day, the pay was somewhat less than $252 million. It is also hard to swallow that the modern-day players choose to ignore the fact that people like Willard's wife, Nancy, might need the raise in pension to their level of compensation to ease any monetary threat caused by the loss of her dear husband. Especially when Willard was one of the players who voted to go back eight years in 1953 and include the players who thought of the pension plan back in 1946.

My day remained glorious and we caught plenty of tuna, but I found it hard fishing with tears in my eyes.

Willard Nixon

My Surfing Days

Some things in life are worth doing over and over and over again. Riding an ocean wave on a surfboard is at the top of the list. It is a thrill never dulled. Every wave is different not only in size, but in shape, and a skilled rider stands out like a beacon. I was an avid surfer but my lighthouse wasn't always visible.

At the age of 34 (1964), I decided to learn to ride a surfboard and started the considerable task in front of the Kauai Surf Hotel on Kalapaki Bay. My mentors were young high school kids like Carlos Andrade, Jimmy Anakalea, Bobby Kama, "Hawk" Kawaihalau, "Squeekie" Kealoha, Albert Kong and most of them agree the Hawaiian term "Dumb Haole" came from those sessions of one pearl dive after another. (Write for explanation.)

The famous big wave rider, Titus Kinimaka, was 9 years old and I finally offered him money to stop "hanging ten" on the shore break while I staggered out of the water, totally spent and plopping face down in the sand. There were days when I barely reached the swimming pool bar where Mabel (long time bartender) would pour me a lethal Mai Tai to get my heart started again. She once told me that the kids were worried I would hit a parked car over by the wall.

One of the problems in my quest to ride waves was my size. The surfboards I rented simply were not big enough, which made it doubly hard to catch a wave when I started. I finally flew to Honolulu and found a board more my size. It was made by Hobey Alter and was 12' long and 24" wide. I am proud to say that this board was on one great wave after another, unfortunately, some of the time I wasn't on it. I was swimming after it. Those were the days of no leg leashes.

Another great problem that all surfers inherited, in the days before leg leashes, was barefoot reef walking. Almost all good waves, with consistent rideable shape, break over shallow reefs and a riderless surfboard inevitably winds up there. The waves that break on living coral reefs are the toughest by far as the sharpness takes its toll. Sharks, being attracted to blood, gave me an advantage at those places. I would be surfing without a crowd, because I was almost always bleeding a little.

There is a great deal of timing and technique in the moment of transition from prone paddling to standing and, only after hours of practice is this moment mastered. Even then, without the physical conditioning to get the board moving forward at the speed of the wave, it is useless. Therefore, I had to get in good physical shape. The old line, "I don't jog because the ice cubes keep bouncing out of my glass," fits me perfectly, but it had to be done and was a task well worth it.

How did I rate as a surfer you ask? The kids said I was a wonderful swimmer.

Let's go Duck Hunting

The one hunting trip that stands out glaringly in my mind was in 1954 with my sister's husband, Don, when we went to Big Bear Lake, California to go duck hunting. Neither one of us had ever been duck hunting. What duck license?

We left after dinner from Van Nuys and while driving through the desert around Victorville that night, we stopped to shoot jack rabbits. I believe we slept in the car at a boat rental dock at Big Bear and were out on the lake very early with a 14' boat with a 18hp outboard, one case of beer and one single shot shotgun.

It was a glorious crisp and clear morning at that 6,000ft + elevation, but we were not the first out on the lake and could hear, now and then, the sound of gunfire. Damn, this was great! Don, with gun in hand, sat up on the bow and I ran the boat. I had that beauty going wide open when we spotted the first flock of ducks sitting in the water at the end of the lake up toward Big Bear City, where there were no other boats. I steered straight for them and, as they lifted off the water in flight, Don let go a blast. Nothing fell. Not to worry, we had plenty of gas and ammo and I swung the boat around and gave chase as the birds were now heading for the other end of the lake.

Without regard to the noise we were making with our shouts and motor noise or the wake of our boat, Don and I were now locked into the pursuit and destruction of those feathered suckers. We could have cared less about a number of guys sitting in boats with their engines raised out of the water (clue) giving us the "up your bucket" sign.

One guy in particular was unique. He was in a kayak and kept waving at us as we sped by, firing at the now hated ducks. What made him unique was the fact that he kept waving for us to come to him.

At that point, the thing hurting the constant pressure duck attack was that we had to stop to relieve ourselves constantly and the case of beer was running low, possibly affecting our aim. We never did hit or even cause a duck to swerve.

Then I made the mistake of saying, "You think that guy in the kayak is in some sort of trouble Don?" He replied, "I don't know Frank, let's see." As we approached him, we were shocked to see a badge on his jacket and hear him scream, "Both you rotten sons-of-bitches are under arrest!" I looked at Don and then back at the officer and said, "Sir, I think we are only under arrest if you have a motor in that kayak."

He didn't and the two rotten sons-of-bitches went throttle wide open to the boat rental dock, paid cash and were gone.

Don and the London Bar Maid

When I think of laughs I always think of 1997 in London with my brother-in-law, Don. With our wives we had boarded a double decker bus and were glad we did because our announcer tour guide turned out to be simply wonderful. An actor by night, the man was flawless in his presentation and his humorous asides were belly laugh stuff. In fact we hated to get off the bus, but we did to tour the Tower of London which, by the way, isn't a tower at all; it's a castle with a very bad reputation. In the old days, many visitors wound up in the moat minus their heads. After touring the place and seeing where Sir Walter Raleigh (like I cared) spent his last days, our wives decided to stay and look at the crown jewels which were in another building within the walls, but since the jewels weren't mine, I opted to jump back on the next bus with Don and go find the Imperial War Museum across the river Thames.

The nice thing about the tour buses in a lot of the great cities is the fact they are a one-ticket-per-day-deal and you can get on and off as you please along their specific route. The closest this bus got to the museum was about five city blocks and at that point, Don and I hopped off and started the considerable walk in pleasant sweater weather. Pleasant or no, we started to heat up and after a few blocks we decided to jaywalk to get to the side of the street that the museum was on. Lo and behold! There was a pub in our way. Imagine that!

It felt good to sit down and after looking around, it was agreed the joint wasn't "five star" but it was clean and the beer mugs looked washed, so we proceeded to have two pints of Guinness brought to us by a rather stout middle-aged woman. She wasn't hostile at all but it was obvious the place didn't get many strangers.

I was on Don's left sitting at the bar side by side and off to our left a young man and a girl were playing pool on a standard slate table of great weight that returned the pocketed balls to a collection tray by way of under-table chutes. I didn't give the scene a second thought and continued to enjoy the moment until the young man called to the barmaid, "Hey Mum! A bloody ball is stuck again!"

Without a moment of hesitation, our barmaid went out from behind the bar over to one end of the pool table, got into a weight lifter's stance and with a great grunt lifted the table enough to get the lone ball rolling down the chute to the collection tray. She then returned behind the bar as if nothing had happened.

"Good God Almighty," I whispered as I turned to look at Don, "Did you see that?" Don just stared straight ahead as if in shock. He remained silent for some time so I asked, "What are you thinking?" Don turned to face me and soberly said, "I'm thinking we better leave this woman a damn decent gratuity."

Kea

Carl Matsumura is a rare man who I call on a lot to find out how to do things because he has a gifted way of explaining how something should be done.

Then there is Kea Sullivan. This 10-year-old has made my life a joy when she is here. She is always "up," always easy, always smart and caring and, most of all, never goes past me without a smile or a hand slap or a hug. It's just too good!

She and I went to breakfast today because she was with us last evening at Carl's place for the annual Mochi Pounding Party (which I intend to never miss if invited) and while sitting with a brew in hand and watching the event, she came over and sat down next to me. I asked her how she liked it. She said, "I am really bored Gramps!"

I suppose watching guys pounding the cooked rice with long hau bush wood headed hammers (always new) into the stone bowl doesn't necessarily move a young girl and when they take the pounded mass to the table where the gals shape it by the handful into a cookie shape and stuff it with different kinds of condiments, it may seem like it happens every day to her. It takes a long day to pound enough rice to satisfy all the people they invite to watch the tradition and lend some muscle to it. In the end everyone gets a plate of the great effort to take home just before the real party starts.

I said to Kea, "Bottom line girl, is that you're out of luck because your parents and your grandmother and I aren't bored but I will try and make it up to you at a later date." She suddenly brightened and said, "How about taking me to breakfast tomorrow at Dani's Restaurant Grandpa?" "You're on girl!" was my response.

Well, I don't "Indian give" my word and next morning to Dani's I staggered but I have never been prouder of being with anyone. She acknowledged the people she knew by a small wave and smiled at me constantly. I was wordless as she told the waitress she wanted two eggs over easy with two scoops of rice and a side order of crisp bacon. We waited a long time for the food to arrive but there wasn't a time I felt uneasy because of the wonderful demeanor this young lass can make happen. She smiled a lot and looked me in the eye as if to make me feel good. She let me know she was happy to be there with me without saying it. Are you getting my message here?

I intend to make sure she goes with me every year to Carl's. I hope it remains so boring to her that I have to take her to breakfast anywhere she wants to go to make up for it. This coming year I will insist Carl goes with us too. After all he has created the problem!

Switch

And now, 11 years after granddaughter Kea, there is Kapono Sullivan. The minute he arrives the voice pitch rises in our home. Pono in Hawaiian means to "do things right." Hopefully, as the voices start to lower in pitch, someone will explain to the lad that living up to the name is paramount and if he fails to do so, he may have to suffer like his father and his father and his father, etc.

In today's world, putting a hand to a child's butt is said to be out of line. I wish it were while I grew up, but as I look back on it now, I realize my father never beat me long with that flat, thin, narrow, strip of wood that stung like a barrel of bees. It only took about two of those beauties for me to re-think the events leading up to my getting called to the cellar where punishment could be muffled. I can also attest to the fact that the learning curve was instantly elevated and greatly enhanced in those sessions. "It would be stupid of you to do this again boy" are the words he would use as the ritual came to an end.

At times, when my mother had ordered the ritual, my dad would say, "Holler loud" and he would hit the stair post and you can bet I hollered loud. Then I made the mistake one time of thinking he let me off because he didn't care what Mom wanted. The learning curve went straight up again!

It was never savage and mostly one whack did the trick, but if I resisted he would calmly explain he would have to give me a second one because I wasn't acting like a boy should who was clearly guilty. "You knew from the beginning you were doing what you shouldn't be doing. You knew from the very start where it all would end if you were caught or kept it up. I don't like this any more than you do boy but bad behavior is unacceptable in this house." And so it was. And so, I hope it will be, as this family starts to bring a young healthy boy "up to speed" to become a productive, caring, proud, reasonable human being.

My sister, Carol, says, "I remember one time I was sitting on one of the stairs and Dad was standing in front of me with tears in his eyes. I don't remember if he actually hit me or not. I think Mom came to the door and said, 'have you spanked her yet?'"

When Kapono's father got out of hand I would take him into his room, make him take his pants down and give him a bare hand whack. Later, when he got too big for that sort of thing, I wrote letters explaining my position on the matters and put them on his pillow. I heard him say to his mother one time, "Tell him I got the message."

Hey! Pono! When you start hearing lower voices take my advice and do the right thing because there is a history in this family.

The Guinea Pig Business

Before we went to California on August 24, 2006, Granddaughter Kea and I had a serious discussion about having a mutual pet. I told her that when we got back from the mainland I would accommodate her want and we would get two guinea pigs. She looked at me quizzically and said, "That's great Gramps! What's a guinea pig?" I patiently explained to her that it was a cute little floppy-eared mammal with no tail and didn't bark. I also explained that when her father was young we had plenty. We quit raising them when my favorite, a red haired dude with long wavy hair, took one little bite out of a deadly oleander leaf.

At any rate, we are back in the guinea pig business and I have built a new "Condoguineaum" to accommodate the two all white, scared to death, very young Guinea Pigs (one male and the other the other) that Mike got free from one of his stevedore friends on Oahu. So, "Hansel & Gretel" came under our control after suffering through a barge ride from Oahu and other ups and downs caused by fork lifts moving the container their cage was in.

The reason Mike had to get them on Oahu is because I went to our one and only pet shop in Lihue and was told they were out of the little devils. Before leaving I asked, "What do the little rascals sell for these days $6.00 or $7.00?" The gal didn't even look up and said, "$46.00 each but that was the last few we had and I can't quote you a price on the next ones we get." I staggered under that news.

Where have I been? Why didn't I monitor the rise in guinea pig prices? I could have been a millionaire by now! Look! I can raise guinea pigs by the thousands by letting guinea pigs do the two things they do best. Number two is eat grass and weeds of which my yard can provide in abundance.

But now Kea is suddenly consumed with a new brother and her competitive swimming and becoming a teenager shortly. She stayed with me today and, in the end, was totally bored. Realizing that 65 years difference of age only works for moments, I damn near cried when she left, but I quickly realized there was an up-side to the event as I would now have total control over the Condoguineaum!

I am back in my world! I can see the future and I'll need some fancy dark glasses to go along with my swagger.

Yes, Kea will probably try and hide her grandfather from inquiring minds but do I care?

Ha! We will see what people think when my chauffeur drives me around to watch over my guinea pig farms.

I always knew I was destined for greatness in some field.

Goodbye to a Good Boat

This morning, February 27, 2006, down at the Young Brothers barge dock, I said a silent goodbye to the 19′ North Carolina dory I built 14 years ago. It is bound for Molokai and will be used down on the east side where it will be perfect because its flat bottom and shallow draft will allow it over the reefs and its high bow will get it home through the afternoon wind that makes waves.

I sold it to Matt Dunbar, the son of a friend for far less than it cost to build just because I know where it's going. This was done because son Mike and I bought a used 17′ Boston Whaler Montauk that out performs, in every aspect, that which my old boat could do.

But it's funny how one becomes attached to things and has a hard time of letting them go, isn't it? Especially since I built the boat myself and now, 14 years later, it was as strong and sturdy as the day it came out of my garage. And for those people who love boats, I can tell you, the bow of that craft remains as easy on the eye as any I have seen.

The thought of building it began as I was in Wilcox Hospital here on Kauai. The bursa on my right elbow had become infected and there was big trouble. I knew if we ever got the arm back that I would have to rehabilitate it. What better way than to build a boat that takes hours of planning that can be thought out while spending 2 weeks in a hospital and the work can re-arm an arm?

Marilyn brought the stuff out of my garage work area to the hospital that I needed to draw on paper the wooden jig to hold firm the stem and keel of the boat so as to maintain the proper angles of the frames and keep the whole thing from torquing as the chines are established under stress on the frames. It was time consuming and perfect for keeping my mind off the damn arm.

Once out of the hospital and feeling a whole lot better, I started the project and as hoped, it was perfect for rehabilitating the arm. I put a lot of thought and hard work into that effort and used only the best materials. The result was very satisfying and I always had a lot of pride in the effort, especially when people down at the launching ramp would come up to me and say they loved the lines of the boat and ask if I built it. (Paint a peacock strutting in your mind here.)

I didn't stay long at the dock this morning and talk with the guys. It was just too painful to look at that labor of love that had been part of my life for so long and now, in essence, I was giving away.

There are a lot of sayings about boats being a drag until you get rid of them, but here I am 76 years later thinking I couldn't live without one.

Sunset

Among my other duties running the Beach Service at the Kauai Surf Hotel in 1966-67 was captaining the 41' sloop-rigged catamaran on the Sunset Sail out of Nawiliwili Harbor. I would drive our 35 passenger bus from the hotel to the docks with a quiet and completely in control group of strangers enjoying their vacation. On return, I would bring back a mob of drunk, screaming, friends that inevitably would wait until they reached the carpeted area in the lobby to throw up!

The problem, but also the reason for coming on the sail, was that the Mai Tais were free and there was no limit. One man drank 7 in one hour and I knew he was in trouble when the cigarette he was smoking fell out of his mouth onto his lap and burned a hole in his crotch without phasing him.

Mickey Lake was part owner of the Beach Service and the bartender on the boat. The Mai Tais that Mickey mixed were lethal. In a double Old Fashion glass were two shots of 80 proof rums with the mix and a 1/2 inch of 150 proof Lemon Hart rum floating on top with the normal fruit and miniature umbrella. One was enough to make the sail smooth no matter what the ocean was like. Two and the group would be looking for whales to harpoon. Three and everyone wanted to sail in front of the hotel and moon the people having cocktails in the Planter's Bar.

Mickey's bar was down in the right side hull and the drunker the ride got the further back in the hull he would move. But good kid here had to stand and steer in their midst and be sober! I would talk with the group and explain what they were seeing. "The lighthouse we are passing is no longer manned and is fully automatic," I would explain. The reply might be, "What lighthouse? Christ's sake, I can't even see the front of the boat!" Why no one ever got hurt on that boat I will never know.

Getting the boat back to the dock was tricky enough, as it was a downwind approach and a cross wind landing. I had to do it many times without the aid of a very faulty auxillary outboard motor. The real problem though was getting the people off the boat once we were tied up to the dock. Because of the old tires attached to the pier, there was an 8" gap between the dock and the boat when we had it all secured. Nevertheless, we had them up to their thighs in that narrow slot many a night. One night while getting off, a lady grabbed my collar and while I tried to help her stumble off the boat she tore the front of my shirt off.

To this day, whenever I see someone drinking their second Mai Tai, I wait patiently to see the first sign of their recognition that shortly they will have to look into their wallets to find out who they are.

Warner

The sun rises vertically 22 degrees 26 minutes north of the equator in the summer and then goes 22 degrees 26 minutes south in the winter. There are 60 minutes in a degree and a minute is a mile. Therefore, Lihue, Kauai lies 1,346 miles north of the equator right on the 22 degree parallel. Look, I am not talking about which way the water rotates as it is flushed down the toilet here! I am trying to tell you people that when you are as close to the equator as we are, you...

OK, forget the above! What I'm trying to tell you is that it should not have been as cold as it was one Saturday evening when Marilyn and I arrived for dinner at Ernie and Joan Warner's home in Koloa. Cocktails were served as we came through the door and we lifted our glasses to the winter sunset along with any other damn thing that seemed to be appropriate. This took a little time and we may have had more than a couple of drinks. Joan put together an excellent meal and afterward we retired into the living room where a fire was crackling in the massive river rock fireplace to keep out the rare but very cold night air on the island.

Ernie Warner was the harvest boss at Grove Farm on Kauai when Grove Farm was in the sugar business and a very articulate, interesting and thoughtful 6' 7" man. I liked him the moment we met and nothing has changed to this day.

Therefore, after dinner, when Ernie offered another "zip" I said "how nice." Later it was, "What about a 'touch,' Sully?" "Of course, my friend." The conversation continued to flow as time ran out on a great night. Unfortunately, the booze ran out too, but Ernie was adamant that one more for the road not be just the name of a song. So the two of us scoured the depths of their kitchen and found a bottle of Kirsch left over from a fondue party. He looked at me. I nodded. He poured us a "pop" on the rocks. It was then I knew that Warner could acquire the taste of lizard urine if challenged as he seemingly enjoyed the last sip of that mistake. It was awful. It tasted like the squeezings of a used Brillo pad. Well yes, I did finish mine but what could I do? Insult a pal? No way! Even though I risked being a commode-hugging drunk.

Somehow the decision to end the evening was reached. You have to give the gals credit for that. Goodbyes were tendered and, as a final parting shot, Ernie said, "I really like your shirt." That was good enough for me. I took it off and gave it to him on the spot!

Driving the 20 minutes home, I started to shiver badly and said, "Jesus, Marilyn, I am freezing to death!" Her reply has worried me to this day. "Of course you're freezing you damn fool, you're lucky he didn't say he liked your slacks too!"

Kipu

Carl Matsumura came into the yard trailering a small backhoe and dug out the cave-in hole next to our 36-year-old cesspool to make it bigger to afford a footing to support the re-bar he drilled into the sewer cap. He hand dug the shape he wanted and set the re-bar and tie-wired it. He supplied the re-bar and did the drilling, cutting and bending. When son, Mike, and Mike Matsumura (Carl's nephew) got off work at Young Brothers just before noon, our Mike picked up 15 more bags of Quikrete to add to the six in my garage and Mike M. towed the big mixer up from Carl's warehouse and put it in place. Uncle Kelvin joined us and the concrete was poured and all I had to do is backfill and grass it. Cost was six Burger King Whoppers and a few beers plus $75.00 for the cement.

There are no words when it comes to my admiration and friendship with Carl. The trouble is it all keeps coming my way with nothing going his and I find myself feeling guilty because of all the things he has done for me and the wonderful times in which he has included my family and me.

Just last week he was taking Elton Tanaka in to see Kipu Kai for the first time and asked if I'd like to trail along. I've been there many times by boat and pickup truck but you can never see enough of that place.

After negotiating the steep one-lane road and stopping at the caretaker's house to announce our arrival into that totally isolated 300-acre private place, we continued down to the water in four wheel drive in sandy conditions. Once there, Carl led Elton down the beach where he has had some luck and Elton put in a damn good hour of casting. Elton (retired Sears executive) is no slouch at fishing and can play golf like a pro while being a wonderful guy to be with.

As for me, I wasn't about to walk that far with no fishing rod and took a seat on a huge log in one of the most peaceful environments left in this world. We were, as usual, the only humans on that 3/4 mile crescent stretch of sand surrounded by steep cliffs. I sat there alone reflecting on all the wonderful things I have been privy to in this life and all the things I look forward to. Just like when I pitched, I won't quit. Someone will have to take me out when they can't stand what I am doing. Getting old is to be avoided at all costs and that takes a mindset of never giving up.

Carl is one of the reasons I will never quit because I would be afraid of disappointing him.

Busy Signal

For some people, the telephone is a convenience for a brief message. On the other hand there are those folks who tend to go on and on and, yes, on.

One of the reasons my marriage to my wonderful wife has endured is because I am not the kind of person who would tell you which of the above she represents. Although I will tell you, she is not of the first.

Take for instance the day she had to take me to work because my truck was in the repair shop. I had a good day running the golf operation for the Westin Kauai Hotel and about 4:30 PM, I phoned home from the pro shop intending to ask her to come and pick me up. The phone was busy. No matter, I needed to go to my office before going home anyway. My office was through the lobby of the complex that housed the Terrace Restaurant (casual dining), the bar, the health centers (men and women), the Masters Restaurant (formal dining), the Tennis Pro Shop, and down a number of steps to the level of the outside health pool. There, I put my desk in order and called home again. It was busy.

Not wanting to stall around there, I proceeded around the corner passing by the tennis courts and down steps, across the cliff cottage road to the elevator that goes down to the beach. Once at the beach promenade, I proceeded to the pool bar for a beer. I put the beer away in no time, as a guy finds loitering around that pool very difficult due to some of the female guests walking around in bathing suits made with less cloth than would suffice for a blindfold. I used the phone, but my number was BUSY. OK. I might as well walk to the end of the promenade across the bridge to JJ's Broiler. After another beer I called and, yes folks, same #%&*.

Trying now to keep control, I thought, "best keep walking instead of staying here, drinking another beer and be mad in public." So, off I go out of JJ's turning left past all the shops, across the street to the beginning of Lala Road that goes up to the high school. It is at least a 7% upgrade and the temperature is still in the 80s. Passing the high school and getting to the junior high office with the pay phone, I make what is now a plea call. It is useless. On past Pacific Machinery and Nawiliwili Road where, luckily, I was picked up by David Pratt (president of Grove Farm) and he delivered me to my street.

When I opened the door to the house, I heard Marilyn still on the phone. I made myself a drink and sat down. I heard her hang up and when she came into the room she said, "I thought you said you were going to call me to come get you?" And this is really why marriages endure. I replied, "I know my love, but I decided to walk."

My bride Marilyn with our son Mike and with yours truly. If there is a life after death I'm going to wait for this girl, and if she will have me again, eternity will truly be heaven.

Travels with Sauerkraut

When I was dating my bride-to-be in San Francisco, it was my custom to pull out my billfold and say, "When this stuff is gone we go home." Every time I was in that great city, she and I would have a ball. The girl simply had the town wired. She would know a little hole in the wall here where the jazz piano was great. She would know a little restaurant there where the food was so good it made paying the check a pleasure. I had never been around such a vibrant and upbeat gal. Damn it was fun and talk about flattening a few wallets...

Well, over the years not much has changed and if you want to see excitement, just watch my bride in a new city. Hell, watch her in an old city! The result is always the same. We limp out of the places tired, happy and above all, broke.

On one of our trips to Honolulu years ago, we had done our usual thing, like tour the shopping centers for things not available in those days on Kauai. Always a Bloody Mary or two and lunch perhaps at Byron's II at Ala Moana or the Spindrifter out at the Kahala Mall. After a nap, it might have been a couple of Navy grogs and dinner at Don the Beachcomber or Hy's for cocktails and a great piece of meat. Then, at least once on every trip to Honolulu after dinner, we still take a leisurely walk out to the beach bar at the Royal Hawaiian. It remains one of the great places in the world to watch the waves and steal a kiss.

OK, back to the story. After picking up a bag of sauerkraut at a Waikiki deli, Marilyn said, "Call a cab and let's go home." Seemed right to me, but upon checking I found only enough money left to catch the bus, which we did. The trouble was the heat and jostling on the bus rendered the sauerkraut bag almost useless and we were lucky to get on the plane without it spilling all over. Once on the plane, which departed as soon as we got on, I transferred the sauerkraut into one of the convenient bags provided by the airlines on the back of each seat.

Our seats were behind a middle aged couple and, about the time the plane leveled off on its twenty minute flight home to Kauai, I heard the lady say to her husband, "Harry, do you smell sauerkraut?" He didn't reply. "Harry. I smell sauerkraut!" "OK Rose, you smell sauerkraut." There was about a five minute pause and then she said, "Can't you smell sauerkraut Harry?" "Jesus no Rose. What's with the sauerkraut, you ain't pregnant again, are you?" Marilyn and I were giggling so hard we almost had to use another bag.

As we stood up in the aisle prior to leaving the plane, I said in a loud voice to Marilyn who was standing just behind the couple, "I sure wish they would stop shipping all the sauerkraut to Kauai by plane."

Thrills of a Lifetime

My very first thrill was throwing a rock and hitting what I aimed at. I was 4 years old. I remember it very well because the thing I hit ran home and told his father.

When I was six, I could hardly stand it, knowing I was to travel by car from Burbank to Sacramento with my father (just the two of us) overnight in a convertible Dodge with a big wooden steering wheel to see his mother.

My cousin's husband, Bob Pfieler, took me on one summer as a preferred laborer on his 100-acre ranch when I was 12. I shot my first gun there. I learned to drive there. He put me on his brand-new tractor and showed me how to rake lima beans into windrows for the harvester, and then left me by myself to do it. I fell into bed every night totally spent and excited about the next day.

I remember the excitement I felt the first time I put a face mask on and dove underwater to the beauty and mystery of the sea.

The first outside loop in an open cockpit biplane got my attention big time.

When the Golden Gate Bridge appeared out of the fog to welcome me home from the war, I couldn't stop smiling with the excitement of being alive.

Almost nothing can compare with walking off the field after pitching nine innings and winning in the Major Leagues.

Taking off on a 15-foot wave and having to wait until the surfboard gets to the bottom before you turn along the giant wall of water will test your veins.

I was at the wheel of a 57-foot sloop all day roaring across the Kauai Channel from Oahu to Kauai with the boat at hull speed and beyond in 18-foot breaking seas. It was exhilarating!

While skiing, I took a wrong turn and found myself on a double black diamond drop in Vail, Colorado. I found I could use the same term as I used while playing golf, Oh Shit!

Now, 72 years after that first thrill, I get the biggest bang out of being offshore with a cold can of beer looking for a pile of birds swooping over a school of fish.

Although, flying First Class with my bride on "Virgin Atlantic" to London with my sister Carol and her husband Don, gets the blood moving nicely.

I've had a magical ride but, the best was when I waited alone in the bar on Powell Street under the St. Francis Hotel in San Francisco. It was 1960 and I wish you could have seen the way this girl looked when she came in there. I think we dined at the Owl & Turtle in North Beach. The way she looked didn't betray the way she was or still is. My heartbeat has never been the same.

Moments to Remember

Looking back, there have been moments in my life that can't be erased, but I sure as hell could have done without them.

I remember standing with my pants and undershorts at my ankles in a large gym in downtown Los Angeles among at least 150 guys that showed up for the physical to enter the Army draft in 1950. We all stood there baring our units (in some cases shortcomings) while a doctor, escorted by a U.S. Army sergeant, checked one and all for hernias. Never understood why the MD kept smiling the whole time while the sergeant had a look of, "How the hell did I get this job?"

I could have done without Stan Musial jumping on one of my high fastballs to end the 1955 All-Star game.

I will always remember the bad moment I had at 5:30 one grey and windy morning aboard Goodale's 55ft fishing boat "Kamanu." The night had been black and there had been no sleep because we had struggled to see South Point passing Niihau on the all-night run from Nawiliwili Harbor to Kaula Rock. Hobey Goodale was at the helm. The wind was 25 knots and the sea about 12 feet. I was sitting on the deck of the bridge behind him leaning against the inside bulkhead. It had been a down-wind trip which means we had been inhaling diesel exhaust the whole 70 miles and, to be honest, I thought the morning couldn't get any worse when David Goodale (Hobey's son and captain of the boat) struggled up the ladder to the bridge and plunked down beside me. In his left hand was a kim chee sandwich that was dripping down his arm and in his right hand was a beer!!!!!!!

There have been some people I have worked for who have seen their role in this life as superior beings. Those times took their toll despite my rationalizing. One in particular stands out. He was an English major and insisted on only talking through memos. His first act was to correct the memo with a red pen and not until it was corrected by me would he read it for content!

Korea was a place and time that I didn't need, then again, all wars are.

But, the all-time bad moment came when Wally Wallace had a golf tournament at the Kiahuna Golf Course in Poipu, Kauai. It was a typically Wally inspired "Big Golf" tournament and on every hole there was a different rule. The first hole had to be played from the tee while standing on a mattress. I was surrounded by at least 35 guys when I hit one of my all-time good drives. There was actually applause until my wife Marilyn, who just happened to be going by to her assigned tee with her three playing companions, shouted out, "Hey Frank! That's the best thing you have done on a mattress in three years."

My Diamonds

I have never been a jewelry man. That said, Kauai, when I first arrived in February of 1964 was glittering like a diamond and for a very long time very little changed in my eye as more than half my life has been spent on this small piece of spectacular earth. I admit to be rooted like an oak tree.

Building a house that visually welcomed the highlands and cloud-filled vistas created a place of rest for me that still warms my soul. Our north-facing picture windows are alive with endless cloud formations that drift over the highlands creating moving shadows that make a movie theater out of our living room.

Living on an island takes a special breed. The fact that I found a girl who willingly wanted to share the adventure and steadfastly held her ground when times were tough is remarkable and makes the present even sweeter.

Even today (2007), life is easy here on Kauai. It has its own challenges, but nothing like mainland living. Getting through a day here is a lot easier because of the minute distance we have to travel, and the weather is outstanding if you like short pants and cotton shirts and wonder why socks were invented.

In the 17 years I traveled (baseball, Army) I remember being unsettled in the big cities because I felt there was something going on that I was missing, but every visit to an island put that feeling to rest. Once island-bound I have always had this great peace come over me that in essence says, "You're home. Nothing is going on that you're missing. Relax."

In the 43 years we have been on this best of all islands, I have had few yearnings to go elsewhere and still don't, but times have changed here as they do everywhere that people want to live. Our population has exploded and most of the newcomers are very rich people. Million-dollar houses are going up like popcorn heated and causing land values and traffic to escalate to a ridiculous level.

I have no idea where it all will lead but Kauai is no longer a place I would move to if I were a young man. It is too busy, too populated and too expensive. Where would I go? I don't plan to waste a moment researching it. Hey! This is my island! And besides, I am too old to go anywhere and this has been and will be my final stand. Never lost with me is the fact I worked for five different companies over a 40-year span within two miles of my home and lived with the woman I have loved from the day I met her.

Even though I'm not a jewelry man, I admit to having two sparkling things that I will never part with.

A MOMENT IN TIME

The next few pages will explain the two pictures above.

Back to Fenway

It all started when the Boston Red Sox came under new ownership and created a first-class publication just for us old-timers. I was touched, and when Herb Crehan, the gifted portrait writer for the Red Sox and author of the new book out, "Red Sox Heroes of Yesterday," put his words to my career, I was impressed.

After 45 years I felt back in the fold, especially after Debbie Matson (director of publications) was so up front, caring and sincere with our dealings.

So I started thinking about a return to Fenway Park and what it would be like to watch my first live baseball game since I was with the Minnesota Twins in 1963. I asked my wife, Marilyn, what she thought about going back, forgetting that her best friend, Gayle Kattar, lives there and couldn't believe the quick, "You bet!" We even bought tickets to a game but my health had a hiccup and cataract surgery resulted in the bad news that I lost the sight in my right eye with the good news being that my golfing buddies were now only half as ugly.

Then my ticker needed a piece of metal pipe. The good news was that I felt better. The bad news is I have to be searched at airports. At any rate, we cancelled the trip but I kept seeing e-mail correspondence between my wife and Gayle who never abandoned the project and acted as if it was just a setback in time.

Then came the e-mail from Debbie Matson who said the Museum of Fine Arts in Boston was about to honor the great illustrator, Norman Rockwell, and since it was the beginning of the baseball season they would be featuring "The Rookie" picture that was on the cover of the Saturday Evening Post (1957). She said they wanted to know if I had any memorabilia around the house from that experience that I might loan them. I thought about it for a while and then it dawned on me the only thing I had laying around the house concerning that picture was me! I also realized I was the only living ballplayer left in that artwork and, in essence, would have no critics! Marilyn! Mortgage the house! We've got to go!

5/3/05

We board a plane to Honolulu, then board a plane to San Francisco and stay what's left of the night.

5/4/05

At dawn we board a plane to Minneapolis, then board a plane to Detroit, then board a plane to Manchester, New Hampshire. Are you kidding me? No! In Minneapolis I thought we were walking to Detroit because our departure gate was so far away. When you book on the spur of the moment the airlines have you at their mercy. They have none! Ah, but getting off in Manchester we are met by Richard and Gayle Kattar and after an easy ride to their wonderful home in Tyngsboro, Massachusetts, we are in a warm loving atmosphere that makes it all worth while.

Let me stop here and tell you about our host because he should be more well known throughout our land of freedom. Richard Kattar's resumé, in a small section on page 2, has this modestly listed:

Military awards: 2 Legions of merit. 5 Bronze Star medals for Valor. 9 Air Medals for Valor. 2 Meritorious Service Medals. 2 Army Commendation medals. Vietnamese Medal of Honor. Vietnamese Gallantry Cross with Cluster. Conducted briefings for the Vice President of the United States, Secretary of State, Secretary of Defense and the Secretary of the Army. He also commanded Fort Devens.

The only thing Richard and I have in common is a Combat Infantry Badge. Yet I bask in his hospitality. The man is unique. We talked of many things and every time I was awed at the direct thoughtful reasoning he is able to bring to a subject. To think I can call him a friend is as good as it gets.

5/5/05

Vesper Country Club (the Kattars are members) is the fourth oldest in the U.S. It dates back to 1875. We play this terrific layout in perfect weather with no one around. Is this OK or what? A couple of beers and lunch and I am as happy as a bull dog on a meat wagon. We go back to the house and the bull dog takes a big time nap. We have dinner in the formal dining room along with the Papendorps and the Olsens and make it vibrate like a sound stage with laughter and chatter. I may have gone to bed with one shoe on.

5/6/05

Woke up to rain and cold temperatures but I hadn't anything planned so no big deal and that evening the Kattars take the Olsens and the Sullivans to the club for a very impressive dinner. I forego the karaoke in the basement after we get home. Look! I've already lost an eye, why lose an ear?

5/7/05

Richard is teaching a class at Boston University, but in his home the preparations of a gala party were underway. The theme was centered around the Rockwell picture of "The Rookie" and Red Sox stuff was everywhere. Hard to believe you can find a Red Sox tablecloth but there it was. I kept myself busy in my best position in life. I had a Sam Adams and criticized everyone.

Talk about a party. It was simply a smashing success. Thirty-some people can't get along any better and before I knew it the hours had raced by. I got to meet Herb Crehan finally and, the minute I did I knew, I would be comfortable with the talented man.

I'm pretty sure I talked with everyone who showed up and unfortunately found I was the only suspect.

5/8/05

We all loll around and eat lobster and leftover party food so the girls don't have to cook on Mother's Day. I thought it was big of us males.

5/9/05

Richard, Gayle, and Marilyn drop me off in Kenmore Square right in the area of the old Kenmore Hotel (no longer there) where I stayed many times.

I don't know why but I wanted to be alone when I walked to the ballpark. So when I kissed Marilyn goodbye I felt guilty as hell, but I know, after living with the girl all these years, that she'd understand more about it than I.

I checked into the new, very upscale Commonwealth Hotel and got to my elaborate room about 1:30 PM. Opened a can of beer out of the stocked bar and let my memory engage on years ago and how it was to be the starting pitcher at the place I was about to see once more. I used my pen to put some thoughts on paper and when the beer was gone, I lay down on the bed and fell sound asleep. I woke up about 1 ½ hours later and felt like a million dollars. I was ready to re-enter the past for a moment in time.

College kids were everywhere in Kenmore Square when I went out the door held open by the doorman. Even at 3:30 PM (game time 7:00 PM) the Red Sox fans were coming out of the "All Trains" tunnel just doors down from the hotel entrance and drifting down toward Brookline Avenue. I followed and as I walked over the freeway bridge, I remembered the bridge spanned the railroad tracks back then. Man! This was great! It was the same walk I did time after time. On days that I pitched, since I didn't have to be there early, I walked that very path with people who would be unaware I was struggling to stifle adrenalin because I was about to be one of the main figures in their entertainment package.

After crossing the bridge I looked up to my left going across Lansdowne Street to see the back of the left field wall and saw the new $100 seats that are atop that old structure. Reaching Yawkey Way, I kept walking down to the Concession Entrance and tried to con my way into the park with my "Lifetime Major League Pass" (good for entry but no seat) past a young guy who politely informed me with a smile, "Not a chance!" I didn't waver and walked another twenty feet to the "Press and Media" entrance and flashed the same metal card and a much older man stood up, shook my hand and said, "Welcome back Sully." It was then my latent ego started to stir.

I walked in underneath the stands turned right toward the home team locker room and I mean to tell you it hasn't changed a bit! I broke off the walk to the locker room to go up a tunnel to the field and there it was! Fenway Park in all its glory.

Damn, it was just like I remembered. I must admit to wiping my one eye. It was then I knew why I wanted to do it alone. There is no way I could have defended my tearful emotions at this poignant moment for me.

After watching batting practice for awhile it was time for me to go back outside and find Herb Crehan as he had invited me to sit with him. We had decided to meet at Brookline Avenue and Yawkey Way and, true to his word, he was there.

Herb and I had been corresponding for months and I already liked the man before I met him at the party so I felt completely at ease as we waited for the gates to open. When they did we went back into the park and watched some more batting practice and then took the elevator up to the level that the Red Sox Hall of Fame restaurant is on and met our third for dinner, the terrific Debbie Matson. It was great to be with the two people really responsible for my being there. We had a wonderful conversation-filled dinner together in that dynamic setting. I was stoked!

I also got to meet Debbie's boss, Dick Bresciani, who was very complimentary and darn nice to come by and see me. Then Herb and I said our goodbyes to Debbie and walked out to his seats about halfway between the Red Sox dugout and the right field foul ball pole. 35,000+ fans (another sell-out) were treated to a very good rendition of the Star Spangled Banner and the game was underway. No, that's wrong, the "love in" was underway. It was like being at a festival. The crowd was into the thing the minute Tim Wakefield threw his first pitch. They reacted to each out as if it was the end of WWII. I couldn't believe the intensity they all shared and they were up on their feet and down like Jack-in-the-Boxes. I refused to be part of the wave but had to admire their enthusiasm. It seemed to me that it would be impossible not to get jacked up as a player in front of that kind of audience.

About the 5th inning Herb and I walked out to Yawkey Way and I showed the tap man my required identification. He looked at it and said, "You win!" I looked at him confused and he said, "It's the oldest age I've seen tonight so the beer is on me." And damn if he didn't give it to me rejecting the $6 I had in my hand. Was I having a night or what?

I looked around in the 7th inning stretch and didn't see a single person not singing at the top of their lungs "Take Me Out to the Ballgame" but the whole place topped it when they sang "Sweet Caroline" in the 8th inning. Herb left for his home in Natick after that song to beat the traffic, but I was riveted despite the cold. I was comfortable because I had borrowed gloves from Richard and I had purchased a stocking cap with a Red Sox emblem on it. I did it despite the clerk asking the boss if they were still selling them for $15 and the boss said, "No, they are $20 tonight!" Oh, well, I was still up a buck because of the free beer.

Despite the hour, I hated leaving the park. I really had a wonderful time. Herb and I had got along great and the Red Sox were victors. The crowd that had been ecstatic still hummed while slowly moving like contented cows to their mode of transportation. I was totally impressed that 35,000 people could smoothly walk out onto the streets without jostling or any other ugly event. I wandered with them back across the bridge on Brookline Avenue to Kenmore Square. I halted a few moments as a jam of people slowed to negotiate the steps down into the "All Trains" tunnel and then walked on to the entrance to the Commonwealth Hotel and the doorman did his job for a tired, smiling and contented old man.

5/10/05

I am picked up after checking out of the hotel at noon by Gayle and Richard and my bride after one of the best sleeps I can remember. We drive to the foot of the Bunker Hill Monument and enter Warren's Tavern which is the oldest drinkery in the United States and I have the best clam chowder known to man (at least this man). After being insulted by the waitress who said, "What do you expect for $6 ?" when asked if the crab had been forgotten on the crab sandwiches the gals ordered. We laughingly left the joint as friends do who love each other and won't let a stupid moment ruin their time.

After a little nap I was astonished to realize I had slept past the normal start of the adult beverage hour so I got on Gayle's case about not waking me up for that important event. Without hesitation, she responded that the cocktail hour would be extended appropriately, which just shows you why I consider the girl the best hostess in the land. Gayle isn't your normal homemaker. A world traveler and teacher. The wonderful girl is super special.

5/11/05

Gayle, Richard, Marilyn and I hurried to leave for Boston as we had to pick up Elizabeth and Carin (Gayle's daughter and granddaughter) at their home in Somerville and get me to Fenway Park by 10:30 AM. They dropped me off at Yawkey Way and then went searching for a parking spot before lunching at the Boston Beer Works. (I couldn't believe they would go there without me!)

Again on Yawkey Way, I went to the #4 door and entered the start of the stairway that leads up to the Red Sox offices. I explained to the guard at the door that Debbie Matson had asked me if I didn't mind coming in early and sitting in "Autograph Alley" before the game. The guard called her and she and I walked up past the offices and took an elevator to the upper section of the grandstand where she showed me where our seats were. We had 8 seats because Julia and Geoff Sheldon, our close friends from Kauai who spend the summer in Hamilton, Massachusetts, were going to join us.

To be honest, I was somewhat worried that we might be pretty far out in the outfield area but when Debbie said, "Here are your seats, I hope they are OK," I was ecstatic. They were under the roof just behind home plate. I mean they were perfect!

Just another reason to love that girl.

We sat there for a few moments watching batting practice and then walked down to Autograph Alley. Once there, Debbie introduced me to Rod Oreste (manager of publications) who I asked if he thought anyone would come by for an old man's autograph. He smiled and said, "Oh, they'll come by alright."

Autograph Alley is up a ramp to the right after entering the gate. The ramp dead ends and there is a table up there with pictures of old Red Sox players framed on the wall. On the table was a stack of pictures of me and a pen. Not a soul was around to have me sign anything. Then, just about the time I was going to say, "This could be a couple of wasted hours," someone "knocked the top off the ant hill" and a stream of wonderful, polite, smiling people of all ages put me into a writing cramp atmosphere. Two hours later they got the "ant hill" repaired and Rod got me to my seat for the first pitch. Talk about a head swelling event. It was hard to keep my feet in touch with what I was walking on. It's a wonder I didn't have a split lip from smiling that long. New England you are special!

Then, after sitting down in my seat next to Richard, my buddy Geoff, who was sitting about 5 seats away passed along a full cup of beer he had liberated for me. Knowing he wasn't a big baseball fan but being in his debt, I felt the need to inform him what was going on. So I yelled at him, "The guys you see wearing the red socks are the Red Sox." Hey! I owed it to him.

As if the signing wasn't enough, Pam Ganley (coordinator of alumni and archives) came by in the 4th inning and asked me to follow her back up to the press area and there I was asked to sit and comment in the radio booth with Joe Castiglione and Jerry Trupiano on station WEEI for an inning and then was taken to the TV booth for an interview with Eric Frede of NESN-TV. There I also met Dennis Ekersly the Hall of Fame pitcher who I had watched and admired for years. Is this stuff OK or what? As Pam and I left we ran into my old teammate Frank Malzone at the elevator. We jawed at each other and in particular talked of the time he came to the mound in Washington's old Griffith Stadium and he jokingly said, "That's all the ground balls I need. Let someone else have a few." Little did he or I know he had just tied the league record for assists in one game.

Back in my seat with our group, I was trying to explain where I'd been when the 7th inning stretch occured and there was my picture up on the scoreboard and I heard 35,000 people cheer. So I stood up and waved before seeing the TV cameraman that had somehow got into position to our area without any of us seeing him.

Friends, there are no words to explain where my long suppressed ego was going. For those of you who don't have an ego, and I have been in your court for years, I apologize. Actually, as I sit here now and try to put all this to words, I admit to still being elated. It was all so flaming nice.

The closing pitcher for the Sox had problems in the 9th inning and let the lead get away but the captain, Jason Varitek, put his stamp on his status and his name in the record books by ending the game with a dramatic homerun to make the Red Sox victors again and keep my day elevated to the max.

After returning Elizabeth and Carin home we stopped at the Out of the Blue restaurant in Somerville and enjoyed the freshest seafood in town. I slept that night on the very cloud I had been on all day.

5/12/05

As if yesterday wasn't filled with special stuff, this day spilled over the top. Gayle, Richard, Marilyn and I are afforded parking in the "officials only" parking lot at The Museum of Fine Arts. We then enter the giant place and are met by Dawn Griffin (director of public relations) and are whisked to the Bravo Restaurant where I am introduced to the Arts and Science writer for the Boston Globe, Sam Allis. He and I chat for an hour and then he rushed off to meet his deadline. He was a nice guy and reflected it in the article about me the next day in the paper. Trouble was they put a present day picture of me with the piece and little children were scared to go to bed that night all over New England.

Next, Dawn led us down to the area where the original Rockwell painting of "The Rookie" was being displayed amongst a lot of Red Sox baseball memorabilia including Ted Williams' old wire locker. I flashed on it because we all had one exactly like it back then.

The director of the museum, Malcolm Rogers, went out of his way to come down to the area and personally introduce me to the media. We had a great chat and he made me feel special. It was like being let in the front door rather than the side entrance. I was to feel that way the whole time I was there.

Being interviewed in front of TV cameras from three different stations is something I don't do every day here on Kauai so you can bet I tried to watch my lip big time (that's the lip that has been overloading my butt for years) and once through that there were about 10 kids seated next to the painting and I fielded their questions and signed some stuff for them. It all took about two hours and my hat size was going past extra large.

After that was all put to rest, we were taken back up to the elegant Bravo Restaurant and treated to a very special lunch in a very special area with very special people.

Please realize that the folks at the MFA are All-Stars at what they do. They are among the world's best in their profession yet were a delight to be with. To my left was Karen Quinn (MFA curator) then Richard Kattar. Rod Oreste (Red Sox) was on the end. To my right was my bride and then Bill McAvoy (MFA), Debbie Matson and on the end was Herb Crehan. Facing me from left to right it was Gayle Kattar, Dick Bresciani (Red Sox), Dawn Griffin (MFA), Henry Mahegan (Red Sox), Ms. Elliot

Davis (head of the Art of America Department)

The acoustic purity in the room was unreal and everyone at the table could easily be heard. I can't remember sitting at a table with 13 other people being so compatible and caring and I certainly can't remember the last time I sat for lunch with a tie on. The conversation was as easy as the laughter. Although I thought my try at humor failed when I mentioned, "I could have pitched to that armless statue we walked by on our way to this room."

Needless to say the food was wonderful and the chef had gone out of his way with the dessert. Each of us got a plate featuring a chocolate cake home plate with a chocolate bat leaning against it. A ball of some delicious stuff with the seams of the ball painted in chocolate and a few baseball-related edible things making the dish more like a picture. We made sure we took a picture of the plate and then I erased mine. We ended the day in the bookstore area and I signed some of Herb's books while being treated like royalty.

King for a day, a time to remember, a moment in time, take your pick. My ego had just gone 9 innings and won.

Upon arriving back at the Kattar house I got out of the car and walked the garbage cans back up to the house from the street. It had a great settling effect.

5/13/05

Debbie Matson called to ask if she could give Sam Mele the Kattar's phone number as he would like to say hello. Well, I was floored and stammered, "Yes, absolutely, I can't wait!"

Sam Mele was playing first base when I joined the Red Sox. Years later, when I was let go by the Phillies in mid-season, he was managing the Minnesota Twins. I called him for a job and he agreed to let me try out. He gave me the chance and I got by the rest of that season throwing lollipops to the plate but got four wins against one loss.

Sam was the best manager I ever played for. There wasn't a guy on that team who didn't like him. The next year when he called me into his office I said to him, "You don't have to say it, Sam, and I want to thank you for everything." He said he would like me to go out into their Minor League System and teach, which I would have been delighted to do but it had to be OK'd by Calvin Griffin (the owner). I hung around the club for over a week but Griffin, who was in his office daily, ignored my daily calls. So, I left the game and the only thing I knew how to do.

When I heard Sam's voice it made me feel good all over. We talked of old times like when I let the first two batters hit balls off the Green Monster in the final game of the season. We needed to win the game to secure fourth place and a small share of the World Series money. Sam left his position at first base and came up on the mound and said, "Hey! Stop fooling around and get these people out because I need the money." In that game he hit a homerun and we won. We talked of present problems that have chipped away at us but it was all so upbeat I choked when I said goodby. Sam will always be a hero of mine.

5/14/05

Departure day came with the knowledge we have four planes to catch as we follow the sun all the way home. It's back to where the last names are hard to pronounce. Anakalea, Kawaihalau, Waalani, Waialeale. Back to where you are asked to take off your slippers before entering the house and reminded not to take a better pair when you leave. Back to Suemi Okubo's garage with the boys on Wednesday afternoons for the beer and conversation. Back to where I have spent more than half my life. Back to heaven on earth.

But leaving the Kattars and this grand moment in time is not easy. If asked, I will tell you that the devil has just missed his opportunity to ruin the best time I can recall.

SULLIVAN BY THE NUMBERS

L.H. WHITTAKER, JR., QUINCY PATRIOT LEDGER

AP WIRE PHOTO

I hurt my left shoulder swinging at a pitch and Yogi Berra is saying, "Get up you big donkey."

About Frank

Full Name: Franklin Leal Sullivan
Born: January 23, 1930 in Hollywood, California
Bats: Right
Throws: Right
Height: 6'7"
Weight: 215 lb.
Signed: By Boston Red Sox as an amateur free agent in 1948.
Debut: July 31, 1953
Final Game: June 12, 1963

Pitching Stats

Year	Team	G	GS	GF	W	L	PCT	ERA	CG	SHO	SV	IP	BFP	H	ER	R	HR	BB	IBB	SO	WP	HBP	BK	HLD
1953	Red Sox	14	0	1	1	1	.500	5.61	0	0	0	25.2	104	24	16	16	3	11	-	17	0	1	0	-
1954	Red Sox	36	26	6	15	12	.556	3.14	11	3	1	206.1	857	185	72	81	18	66	0	124	1	6	2	-
1955	Red Sox	35	35	0	18	13	.581	2.91	16	3	0	260.0	1,100	235	84	103	23	100	5	129	1	2	1	-
1956	Red Sox	34	33	1	14	7	.667	3.42	12	1	0	242.0	1,048	253	92	112	22	82	6	116	4	8	1	-
1957	Red Sox	31	30	1	14	11	.560	2.73	14	3	0	240.2	961	206	73	76	16	48	4	127	2	7	0	-
1958	Red Sox	32	29	3	13	9	.591	3.57	10	2	3	199.1	836	216	79	91	12	49	0	103	2	3	1	-
1959	Red Sox	30	26	1	9	11	.450	3.95	5	2	1	177.2	751	172	78	86	17	67	2	107	2	7	1	-
1960	Red Sox	40	22	4	6	16	.273	5.10	4	0	1	153.2	678	164	87	94	12	52	6	98	3	6	0	-
1961	Phillies	49	18	19	3	16	.158	4.29	1	1	6	159.1	687	161	76	93	19	55	5	114	1	5	0	-
1962	Phillies	19	0	4	0	2	.000	6.26	0	0	0	23.0	115	38	16	21	2	12	2	12	0	2	0	-
1962	Twins	21	0	10	4	1	.800	3.24	0	0	5	33.1	145	33	12	17	3	13	0	10	1	0	0	-
1963	Twins	10	0	3	0	1	.000	5.73	0	0	1	11.0	49	15	7	7	1	4	1	2	0	0	0	-
Career		G	GS	GF	W	L	PCT	ERA	CG	SHO	SV	IP	BFP	H	ER	R	HR	BB	IBB	SO	WP	HBP	BK	HLD
11 Years		351	219	53	97	100	.492	3.60	73	15	18	1,732.0	7,331	1,702	692	797	148	559	31	959	17	47	6	-

All-Star Games Stats

All-Star Game Pitching

Year	Tm	Lg	GS	W	L	S	IP	H	R	ER	BB	SO	HR	HBP	WP	SB	CS	2B	3B	BK
1955	BOS	AL		0	1	0	3.1	4	1	1	1	4	1	0	0	0	0	0	0	0
1956	BOS	AL	Was selected, but did not play in the game.																	

All-Star Game Batting

Year	Tm	Lg	GS	AB	R	H	2B	3B	HR	RBI	BB	SO	SB	CS	SH	SF	HBP
1955	BOS	AL		1	0	0	0	0	0	0	0	1	0	0	0	0	0
1956	BOS	AL	Was selected, but did not play in the game.															

1955 All-Star Game

American League 5 vs National League 6, July 12, 1955 County Stadium
Attendance: 45,643   Length of Game: 3:17   Umpires A.L.: HP: Hank Soar, 2B: Bill Summers, LF: Ed Runge.
Umpires N.L.: 1B: Al Barlick, 3B: Dusty Boggess, RF: Frank Secory.

Hitting & Fielding Notes, American League

Name	Pos	AB	R	H	RBI
Harvey Kuenn	ss	3	1	1	0
Chico Carrasquel	ss	3	0	2	0
Nellie Fox	2b	3	1	1	0
Bobby Avila	2b	1	0	0	0
Ted Williams	lf	3	1	1	0
Al Smith	lf	1	0	0	0
Mickey Mantle	cf	6	1	2	3
Yogi Berra	c	6	1	1	0
Al Kaline	rf	4	0	1	0
Mickey Vernon	1b	5	0	1	1
Jim Finigan	3b	3	0	0	0
Al Rosen	3b	2	0	0	0
Billy Pierce	p	0	0	0	0
b-Jackie Jensen	ph	1	0	0	0
Early Wynn	p	0	0	0	0
g-Vic Power	ph	1	0	0	0
Whitey Ford	p	1	0	0	0
Frank Sullivan	p	1	0	0	0
Totals		**44**	**5**	**10**	**4**

National League

Name	Pos	AB	R	H	RBI
Red Schoendienst	2b	6	0	2	0
Del Ennis	lf	1	0	0	0
c-Stan Musial	ph-lf	4	1	1	1
Duke Snider	cf	2	0	0	0
Willie Mays	cf	3	2	2	0
Ted Kluszewski	1b	5	1	2	0
Eddie Mathews	3b	2	0	0	0
Randy Jackson	3b	3	1	1	1
Don Mueller	rf	2	0	1	0
d-Hank Aaron	pr-rf	2	1	2	1
Ernie Banks	ss	2	0	0	0
Johnny Logan	ss	3	0	1	1
Del Crandall	c	1	0	0	0
e-Smoky Burgess	ph-c	1	0	0	0
h-Stan Lopata	ph-c	3	0	0	0
Robin Roberts	p	0	0	0	0
a-Frank Thomas	ph	1	0	0	0
Harvey Haddix	p	0	0	0	0
f-Gil Hodges	ph	1	0	1	0
Don Newcombe	p	0	0	0	0
i-Gene Baker	ph	0	0	0	0
Sam Jones	p	0	0	0	0
Joe Nuxhall	p	2	0	0	0
Gene Conley	p	0	0	0	0
Totals		**45**	**6**	**13**	**4**

a: Popped out for Roberts in 3rd inning.
b: Popped out for Pierce in 4th inning.
c: Struck out for Ennis in 4th inning.
d: Pinch ran for Mueller in 5th inning.
e: GIDP for Crandall in 5th inning.
f: Singled for Haddix in 6th inning.
g: Popped out for Wynn in 7th inning.
h: Reached on error for Burgess in 7th inning.
i: Flied out for Newcombe in 7th inning.

Double Plays: Kluszewski-Banks-Robers, Wynn-Carrasquel-Vernon.
Doubles: Kluszewski, Kaline.
Errors: Carrasquel, Rosen, Mathews.
GIDP: Burgess.
Home Runs: Mantle, Musial.
Left on Base: A.L. 12, N.L. 8.
Sacrifice Hits: Pierce, Avila.

Pitching Notes

American League

Name	IP	H	R	ER	BB	SO
Billy Pierce	3.0	1	0	0	0	3
Early Wynn	3.0	3	0	0	0	1
Whitey Ford	1.2	5	5	3	1	0
a-Frank Sullivan	3.1	4	1	1	1	4

National League

Name	IP	H	R	ER	BB	SO
Robin Roberts	3.0	4	4	4	1	0
Harvey Haddix	3.0	3	1	1	0	2
Don Newcombe	1.0	1	0	0	0	1
Sam Jones	0.2	0	0	0	2	1
Joe Nuxhall	3.1	2	0	0	3	5
Gene Conley	1.0	0	0	0	0	3

a: Pitched to 1 batter in 12th inning.
Hit by Pitcher: Kaline (by Jones).
Losing Pitcher: Sullivan.
Passed Ball: Crandall.
Wild Pitch: Roberts.
Winning Pitcher: Conley.

Line Score

All-Star Team	1	2	3	4	5	6	7	8	9	10	11	12	R	H	E
American League	4	0	0	0	0	1	0	0	0	0	0	0	5	10	2
National League	0	0	0	0	0	0	2	3	0	0	0	1	6	13	1

Professional Experience

2005 to present Consultant to Public Bike Path Kauai
1996 - 2005 Golf Consultant to Grove Farm Co.
    Golf Consultant to Casper Golf Management
    Golf Consultant to Koolau Golf Co.
    Golf Consultant to Wailua Golf Course
1992 - 1996 Director of Golf, Grove Farm Co.
    Overseeing Construction of Golf Course
1991 - 1992 Director of Golf, Kauai Lagoons Resort
1988 - 1991 Director of Golf, Westin Kauai
1986 - 1988 Hemmeter Development Co.
    Development of Two Courses
1976 - 1986 PGA Professional, Kauai Surf Resort
    Responsible For All Golf Operations
1967 - 1976 Assistant Golf Professional, Kauai Surf Resort
1965 - 1967 Coast Guard Licensed Catamaran Captain and
    Manager of Beach Services, Kauai Surf Resort
1953 - 1963 Major League Baseball Pitcher
    Red Sox - 8 Years
    Phillies - 1 Year
    Twins - 1 Year
    All-Star Selection - 1955 - 1956
1950 - 1952 Armed Forces
    Infantry Leadership School
    Combat Infantry Badge
    Staff Sergeant

Professional Golfers Association

1980 - 1982, 1996 - 1997, 1999 Board of Directors, Aloha Section
1998 - 1999 Board of Directors, Kauai Junior Golf
1982 Faculty, PGA Business School, Portland Ore.
1981 Faculty, PGA Business School, Kuilima, Hi.

Education

1978 PGA Business Schools I & II
1948 - 1949 University of Southern California
1948 Burbank High School graduate, Student Body President

LIFE IS MORE THAN 9 INNINGS

Index